Dennis McCallum

Walking in VICTORY

BRINGING TRUTH TO LIFE
NavPress Publishing Group
P.O. Box 35001, Colorado Springs, Colorado 80935

The Navigators is an international Christian organization. Jesus
Christ gave His followers the Great Commission to go and make
disciples (Matthew 28:19). The aim of The Navigators is to help
fulfill that commission by multiplying laborers for Christ in every
nation.

NavPress is the publishing ministry of The Navigators. NavPress
publications are tools to help Christians grow. Although publications alone cannot make disciples or change lives, they can help
believers learn biblical discipleship, and apply what they learn to
their lives and ministries.

© 1994 by Dennis McCallum
All rights reserved. No part of this publication may be reproduced
    in any form without written permission from NavPress, P.O.
    Box 35001, Colorado Springs, CO 80935.
Library of Congress Catalog Card Number:
    94-19518
ISBN 08910-98356

Cover photograph: Willard Clay

Some of the anecdotal illustrations in this book are true to life and
are included with the permission of the persons involved. All other
illustrations are composites of real situations, and any resemblance
to people living or dead is coincidental.

Unless otherwise identified, all Scripture quotations in this publication are taken from the *New American Standard Bible* (NASB),
© The Lockman Foundation 1960, 1962, 1963, 1968, 1971, 1972,
1973, 1975, 1977. Other versions used include the *HOLY BIBLE:
NEW INTERNATIONAL VERSION*® (NIV®), Copyright © 1973,
1978, 1984 by International Bible Society, used by permission of
Zondervan Publishing House, all rights reserved.

McCallum, Dennis.
    Walking in victory : experiencing the power of your
  identity in Christ / Dennis McCallum.
      p. cm.
    ISBN 0-89109-835-6
    1. Identification (Religion) I. Title.
BV4509.5.M343   1994
233—dc20   94-19518
                                             CIP

Printed in the United States of America

FOR A FREE CATALOG OF
NAVPRESS BOOKS & BIBLE STUDIES,
CALL 1-800-366-7788 (USA)
or 1-416-499-4615 (CANADA)

CONTENTS

ACKNOWLEDGMENTS

My heartfelt thanks and appreciation go out to my helpers in preparing this book. Aside from the many who have contributed in various ways, I especially thank my readers, Lee Campbell, Dave Norris, Dave and Amy Merker, Martha McCallum, and especially my wife, Holly.

PART ONE

GRACE

WHO ARE YOU?

A few years ago I took my family to the top of the Sears Tower in Chicago. We stood atop this tallest building in the world and looked out over the immense metropolis at night. Through the tinted windows, a city of millions spread out at our feet in an ocean of golden light. The beauty was breathtaking, causing me to marvel at the majesty of the human race. We have certainly done some amazing things. I felt glad to be alive as I sensed my own smallness and realized that the God who created this brilliant race of beings was personally involved with me.

But as I looked down at the beautiful golden ocean of light, I also realized that this vision was very misleading. What seemed so beautiful and cheerful at this height was really an ocean of sorrow and pain. I knew if I could zoom in on the streets of this city, I would see things that would make me shudder in revulsion. We had just driven through neighborhoods that were frightening in their despair: neglected children and brutal gangs of angry youth wandering streets with prostitutes on every corner. The rejection, lack of love, and emptiness in this city (no different from others) would be hard to exaggerate.

THE BEAUTY AND THE BEAST

These two seemingly paradoxical views of the human race are both true. Alongside the wonder and brilliance of humankind is much pain, suffering, and evil. A person would have to be very sheltered and pampered to miss the terrible weight of evil and injustice lying like a smelly wet blanket over our world today. This is the world and the life we have to address unless we plan to act out some phony, fictional form of religious Disneyland.

The Bible accounts for these two aspects of the human race—the beautiful and the grotesque—in a marvelous and consistent way. No other worldview can explain both the majesty and the misery of humans so completely and convincingly as the Bible. Neither can any other worldview give us the means to change, at the deepest level, how our human nature works. Scripture guides us to substantial change that is lasting and real.

We will be looking at God's answers to human nature—your nature—as detailed in Romans chapters 5 through 8. Any Christian who understands and applies this remarkable passage will see exciting change in his or her life—a change not only in outward action but also in inner attitudes and thought patterns. Why not commit yourself before God to invest a few hours to complete this study? As you do, ask God to grant you the full understanding He wants you to have of this vital passage.

GETTING OUR BEARINGS

God has given us many wonderful blessings, and for these we should be grateful. We are right to be thankful for things like our spectacular world, our opportunity to love others, and the chance to live with God forever. But we have to be honest as well as grateful. In our own personal lives we have problems—perhaps known only to ourselves—that are often serious, even devastating. We are also suffering as a result of circumstances outside our control, whether in the past or present.

Then there is one of the most obscene and unnatural of all our problems: death. Why should sophisticated spiritual creatures like ourselves have to undergo such a terrible end? While we should have a grateful attitude toward God, such an attitude shouldn't divert our attention from these problems or minimize their impact on our lives.

Think of some of the questions raised by negatives in our lives:

- ◆ Why do I experience hard feelings like sorrows, envy, or insecurity?
- ◆ Why do I fail?
- ◆ Why are even my best intentions sometimes frustrated by weakness in myself?
- ◆ When I do something nice, why is there so little appreciation?
- ◆ Why does it sometimes seem as if the people around me are so unreasonable?
- ◆ Why do I live my life under the shadow of aging and death?

According to the Bible, before we can appropriate God's answer to the negatives in our lives, we have to come to grips with the negatives themselves. God's answer to our problems has to do with our being "in Christ." But before we can appreciate what that means, we have to understand what it means to be "in Adam." One theologian has expressed this truth this way: Before we can experience God's *yes*, we have to comprehend His *no*.

> *Before we can experience God's yes, we have to comprehend His no.*

START WITH THEORY

The majesty and beauty of the human race are there because we were created in the image of God, and we can reclaim and enhance these traits through the power of God if we receive our new identity in Christ. But the grotesque parts of life are there because of the Fall recorded in Genesis 3. In Romans 5:12 through chapter 8 we read of the close connection between being fallen and being in Christ. The Apostle Paul begins his discussion of spiritual growth in this passage by saying, "Through one man sin entered into the world, and death through sin" (Romans 5:12).

THE ADAM THING—AGAIN?

To many of us, studying passages like this one may seem boring and unnecessary. Unfortunately, such an attitude ultimately leads either to the despair of perpetual infancy or to something worse: Pharisaism.

Anytime we refuse to invest the time and effort it takes to understand difficult background sections of Scripture like Romans 5 and 6, we are unknowingly proposing that we grow spiritually by tinkering with our outward actions while leaving the inside untouched. We would be like children who call to their parents from the wading pool to watch them swim as they hold themselves up with their hands on the bottom of the pool, furiously kicking their feet. The children, of course, are not swimming at all. They are trying to fool their parents, and perhaps even themselves, as they mimic the actions of a swimmer.

This is the way many Christians live their lives. At certain times they become painfully aware they are faking it. And of course, God will usually make certain we have to enter waters too deep for this sort of phoniness. At times like these we find ourselves wondering whether there might be something more, something we missed along the way in the area of spiritual growth.

Such times of undeniable failure can provide an opportunity to finally enter deeply into the meaning of advanced passages of Scripture, like Romans 5 and 6. Failure to do so could keep us from moving on to real maturity in our Christian lives. Like the Pharisees of old, we might plod along, observing any number of spiritual disciplines, struggling to have our daily devotions, wringing our hands through sessions of personal confession of sin, but all the while never really growing closer to God.

THE HEART OF THE ISSUE

What does this have to do with Adam? Just this: Our problem is not only what we do, but what we are.

God is directing our attention to Adam in this key passage because He wants us to come to grips with the way things work in the spiritual realm. Specifically, He wants us to realize that "doing arises out of being."

> *Our problem is not only what we do, but what we are.*

DOING AND BEING

The Apostle Paul writes, "Therefore, just as through one man sin entered into the world, and death through sin, and so death spread to all men, because all sinned" (Romans 5:12). Paul is *not* teaching in this verse that each of us has also sinned in our turn, and so we, too, have to die. On the contrary, the point here is that we all sinned *at the same time* Adam did. This becomes clear in the rest of the passage.

In verse 17 Paul asserts that "by the transgression of the one, death reigned through the one." In other words, it is not by our many individual sins that death reigns, but through *one single sin!* Again in verse 18 he says, "So then as through one transgression there resulted condemnation to all men." It's unmistakable. This passage is teaching that our problem with death and condemnation is the result of Adam's sin. That is why in verse 14 Paul says the problem of sin and death also has effects "even over those who had not sinned in the likeness of the offense of Adam." If there was any doubt, it is removed when we look at verse 19, where he again affirms that "through the one man's disobedience the many were made sinners."

Many of us have heard this teaching before. The Puritans used to teach that "In Adam's fall, we sinned all." But what does it mean, and what's the point for our lives today? The point is vital and essential: *Doing* arises out of *being.* You *do* what you *do* because you *are* what you *are.* Maybe we can remember it if we state it this way: What we *do* arises out of what we *are.*

This is why failure to understand this passage will ultimately lead to Pharisaism or despair. Jesus criticized the Pharisees because they cleaned the outside of the cup, but not the inside (Matthew 23:25). If we focus only on changing our behaviors, we miss the real point. Instead of living out what we *are*, we will be defining our-

> *What we do arises out of what we are.*

selves by what we *do*. According to God, this amounts to the tail wagging the dog. The point is not just that we *do* the wrong thing, but that we *are* the wrong thing!

Imagine an oppressive ruler who ordered his police force to deal totally and permanently with his citizens' misuse of alcoholic beverages. Agents are sent into houses, stores, and bars throughout the country to seize and destroy every bottle of beer, wine, and booze in existence. After an intensive campaign, the police successfully eliminate every drop of alcohol in the country. This illustration (borrowed from Chinese author Watchman Nee) certainly seems like a comprehensive solution! But something is missing. What about the distilleries and breweries that produce the beverages? If these are left untouched, within days millions of bottles will again flood the country.

Of course, no government would ever be stupid enough to carry out such a superficial program. But sadly, many Christians live their lives this way! If we want to get off the treadmill of endless reform programs that seem to go around in circles, we have to come to grips with the issue addressed in this pas-sage: the issue of who we are, of our iden-

> *It's not enough to change what we do; we have to change who we are.*

tity. God wants us to hear something important from Romans 5 and 6: It's not enough to change what we do; we have to change who we are.

AS IN ADAM, SO IN CHRIST

Romans 5:12-21 teaches that we have all inherited a certain identity, a certain nature, from our ancestor Adam. The description of this nature includes the S-word. Though modern people don't want to hear it, the truth is that our basic identity is that of sinners because we are descendants of Adam. One reason this teaching is important is because it explains why, from the cradle on, we experience powerful negatives and uncontrollable urges. We not only received condemnation, but a sin nature too.

Christian apologists are very happy there is a doctrine of the Fall in the Bible because it provides a basis for understanding why evil exists. This is unlike the teachings of most religions, which see no problem with the existence of evil. However, in this study we are not interested in apologetics, because that is not why the Apostle Paul has brought up the fall of the human race in this passage. He has a different reason—namely, he wants us to see, not only what we have inherited from Adam (our identity as a sinner), but also *how* we inherited it (the principle of federal headship). This is the principle we must understand if we are to stop living based only on what we do rather than on what we are.

FEDERAL HEADSHIP

How did we get our fallen nature? What did you or I do to end up in this state? The answer is simple. We were born. There was no decision on our part pro or con. From the first day of our lives we were sinners by nature. Please notice, this truth is taught in numerous other Bible passages, like Psalm 51:5 and Ephesians 2:1 and 3, where Paul says we "were *by nature* children of wrath" (emphasis added).

We don't need to go into great depth about what it means to have a fallen nature right now. It's enough to say our fallen nature accounts for our tendency to rebel against God and authority. It causes us to desire independence in the negative sense of the word—what we could call autonomy, or self-rule. Sadly, our fallen identity also means we are spiritually dead—separated or alienated from God.

Our main concern at this point is *how* we got this nature. Here are a few points to notice, all of which become important later in our study.

- ◆ We were not personally in the Garden of Eden.
- ◆ We did not decide to eat the forbidden fruit.
- ◆ We did not *sense* Adam eating the fruit.
- ◆ We have no tangible experience that confirms our relation to Adam as a federal head.
- ◆ Yet, if we are growing Christians we are obligated to accept God's testimony in the Bible that our identity does indeed find its source in Adam.

THAT'S NOT FAIR!

Does it seem even slightly unfair that we are being negatively affected by a man's decision thousands of years ago? How do I know whether I would have made the same decision if I were there? And even if I would have, shouldn't I be given the chance to blow it on my own behalf? Why is my life being ruined by the choice of another?

These are all good questions. Maybe an illustration will

help us understand the answers.

I come from Scottish stock, and the Scots have a history of violence. Suppose my great-grandpa, no doubt named McCallum, became involved in a duel over the hand of a lady. The duel was between him and another Scot named McClure, and they fired guns at one another to the death. Who do you suppose won such a duel?

The answer is obvious. I wouldn't be writing this text today if McClure had won. Great-grandpa McCallum must have won, because I'm here. In a sense, you could say I won this duel because I was in my grandpa (literally) when he won the duel. Certainly if he had lost, I would have lost with him. I had no choice in the matter. I could not and still cannot feel this victory. Yet here I am, so he must have won the duel (if we suppose such a duel ever happened, which it did not).

It should be clear from this illustration that human choice often affects others, even though they may not agree with the choice or, for that matter, may have had no voice in it. This must be true in many areas. Suppose someone pushed a button launching missiles for a nuclear war. Wouldn't we all be affected even though we weren't involved in any decisions? The awesome power of free choice includes the possibility of choosing something that will result in unfairness to others. This principle is never truer than when dealing with our descendants. My choice of a bride directly affected the genetic makeup of my children, and they had no say in the matter.

It's the same way with our ancestor Adam. What this man did affected him, but it also affected his offspring. Every one of Adam's children inherited his sinful nature. They were born already alienated from God, already determined to do things their way, already sinners. And of course, we are also children of Adam. In a sense, Adam did act for all of us, so there's no need for us to make our own individual choice to rebel from God.

We are rebels by nature, not just on the outside, but in our innermost selves. When we rebel, when we avoid God, we are not acting only outwardly in some superficial way. We are acting out of what we truly are at the deepest level—rebels and fugitives from God. That's why we have no trouble being consistent with a self-centered way of life. All we have to do is follow the course of least resistance, and we will naturally act out what we are by nature. Our *doing* arises out of our *being*.

Because Adam acted for us in this way, bestowing a certain nature and identity upon us, he is called our federal head. Adam stands at the source of a humanity that is the way it is because Adam—our head, our source—acted for all of us. If we accept this proposition, we will see that having a federal head who bestows an identity upon us is very important, either negatively or positively. In our case with Adam, the effect is negative. But there is a ray of hope here as well.

> Like Adam, Christ has also become a federal head.

If receiving our Adam identity leads to a way of life apart from God, a way of life that comes easily and naturally, perhaps this principle can work in a positive direction as well. Anyone who has read ahead in Romans already knows that God has taken exactly this direction in addressing the problems in our lives.

CHAPTER 3

LOSING OUR IDENTITY IN ADAM

Before anything can change on the deepest level in our lives, we have to lose the identity we have in Adam. As long as that identity remains the same, any change in our outer actions doesn't amount to much in the ultimate sense. Losing our identity in Adam is different from losing our sin nature, as we will see later.

Consider our treatments for the common cold. We take nasal decongestants to reduce inflammation. We take aspirin for the headaches and pains. We may even take an antihistamine to dry up our runny nose. But none of these things will *cure* the cold. Such treatments only control the *symptoms* of the cold. That's because there *is* no cure for the common cold! Since we have no cure, we might as well at least try to control the symptoms. We have no better option.

Many Christians have reached the same conclusion about their sin nature. They try different solutions to control the worst of the symptoms of the Adam nature, but none of their measures gets at the source of the problem. This is unfortunate, because with the Adam nature we do have a cure! It's a shame to see people dealing with their sin problems only on the symptomatic level when they could be experiencing real change.

AN IMPORTANT QUALIFICATION

Before going on, we need to make one very important qualification. When we argue that trying to alter our outer behavior is like trying to control the symptoms of a cold, you might conclude that any effort to deal with external behavioral problems is Pharisaism. You might even conclude that efforts in this direction will prevent or block real change based on who you are rather than on what you do. But this would be the wrong conclusion.

There is nothing wrong with controlling negative symptoms.

> *Controlling symptoms is not wrong, but it is insufficient.*

We should find ways to decrease destructive behavior and increase positive behavior in our lives. Behavioral control only becomes a problem when it is the *only* thing we do. It becomes a serious problem when we begin to define our spiritual state by how well the battle with behaviors is going.

To state this differently, the issue is not whether we attempt to control behaviors but how we view that attempt. Do we see controlling our behaviors, or our performance, as either the *definition* of or the *key* to spiritual growth? If we answer "yes" to either of these questions, we have a very serious problem, not unlike that of the Pharisees. On the other hand, there may be certain areas of sin in our lives that need to be controlled in an external way, even though this is not the same as spiritual growth. We need to control some particularly destructive behaviors even if by external means, so they will not block our advancement toward maturity on a deeper level. Controlling negative behavior, while not the same as growth, could be a precondition to growth in some cases.

Let's look at a couple of examples. Suppose you are an alcoholic. Your drinking and your abuse of your family are sinful and destructive. Stopping these behaviors will not make you a mature Christian, but it may nevertheless be necessary to seek control of the behaviors, *even through external means*, like avoiding drinking situations or entering a hospital. Stopping the drinking may open the door for other more complete solutions.

The same could be true of promoting positive behaviors. Suppose you are reclusive. You don't like to go out in the evening, and groups of people make you nervous. In such a state, it may be very difficult to take advantage of Christian fellowship. Unless you find ways to overcome such a reluctance to act, it will be difficult to fully understand God's plan for your life.

Again, a problem arises when the struggle to gain a measure of control over behaviors becomes the defining issue of our lives. It is all too easy to begin to view enhancement of our external performance as being equal to spiritual growth. But even nonChristians change their behavior! Many Hindus and Buddhists undergo disciplines much more impressive than any we are likely to practice. But is this the same as being conformed to the image of Christ? It is not.

THE FATE OF THE ADAMIC PERSON

If we received our identity in Adam simply by being born, how will we ever get rid of it? The Bible is crystal clear on this point: The only possible fate for the person in Adam is death.

> *The only possible fate for the person in Adam is death.*

God will not set about renovating the Adamic person for use in the Kingdom. The verdict of death has already been decreed over this humanity. Romans 5:15 states it plainly: "By the transgression of the one the many died." Elsewhere in Romans this message is repeatedly emphasized. "The wages of sin is death," proclaims Romans 6:23, and we can rest assured, God will not change His verdict. Yet, He is able to tell us in His next breath that "the free gift of God is eternal life in Christ Jesus our Lord."

We already know that Christ bore the penalty for our sin on the cross. This explains why God can forgive us and give us eternal life. But what about the effect of His death in *this* life? How will the death of Christ affect our spiritual growth?

Here is where our study of identity in Adam begins to pay

dividends. Romans 5 and 6 teach that, like Adam, Christ has become a new federal head. This is what the Apostle Paul means in Romans 6:3-4—

> Or do you not know that all of us who have been baptized into Christ Jesus have been baptized into His death? Therefore we have been buried with Him through baptism into death, in order that as Christ was raised from the dead through the glory of the Father, so we too might walk in newness of life.

We saw earlier that the only way to escape the domination of the Adam nature is death. This passage mentions death in the same connection, but with a twist. Here we discover not only that Jesus died in our place but that somehow we died *with* Him.

This passage is teaching that God has declared us to be "in Christ," which, among other things, means we have died to what we were "in Adam." This phrase, "in Christ," is completely different from the statement, "Christ in me." This is what theologians call "identification with Christ." It means God has acted in such a way that we have become *identified with Christ*. Therefore, as far as God is concerned, what is true of Christ's standing has become true of us. Did Jesus die? Then so did I. Did Jesus rise from the dead? Then I, too, rose from the dead. The comparisons can be pressed even further. Did Jesus ascend to the Father in Heaven? Then, according to my identification with Christ, I, too, ascended to Heaven and took my seat at the right hand of the Father! This is expressly stated in Ephesians 2:5-6: "Even when we were dead in our transgressions, [God] made us alive together with Christ . . . and raised us up with Him, and seated us with him in the heavenly places, in Christ Jesus." Of course, we have not become the creators of the world, nor have we become Deity, but the areas where we are identified with Christ are more extensive than many of us would think.

This seems quite abstract. In what sense am I seated with

Christ in Heaven? In what sense am I still seated here on earth? How can God say I died, when I clearly am alive? Wouldn't I have noticed this experience?

USING OUR INSIGHT
We already have the key to answering these questions. That key is federal headship. Adam was our federal head. We didn't feel or sense anything he did. There was no tangible experience on our part. Yet, what we are was directly impacted by this man. First Corinthians 15:45 says, "'The first man, Adam, became a living soul.' The last Adam became a life-giving spirit." Jesus is the last Adam. He is a second federal head. He is called the last Adam because, just as Adam gave rise to a fallen humanity, Christ became the source of a new, righteous humanity. One humanity is doomed to die; the other humanity has already died. One humanity lives in alienation from God; the other is alive to God.

Paul reiterates this in 1 Corinthians 15:21-22—"For since by a man came death, by a man also came the resurrection of the dead. For as in Adam all die, so also in Christ all shall be made alive."

BAPTISM INTO CHRIST
These statements in 1 Corinthians are no different from what we have seen in Romans 6. According to our passage, the key to our new identity is that we have been "baptized into Christ Jesus" (verse 3). This is not referring to water baptism, but to spiritual baptism.

The word *baptizo*, translated "baptize," need not refer to a ritual wherein people are washed or immersed in water. Sometimes the term is used for immersing people into other things. For instance, John said Jesus would baptize people in the Spirit and in fire (Matthew 3:11). Jesus asked James and John whether they were able to undergo the baptism He would undergo, apparently referring to His suffering and death (Mark 10:38). There are other uses of the word as well. It should be clear that the exact meaning of baptism must be determined in each passage by considering the context. The word means "immersion" or a "putting into." But immersion into what?

Here in Romans 6 the apostle is not commenting on our immersion into water, but into Christ. This is baptism by the Spirit. Paul says this "baptism," or immersion into Christ, is an integral part of becoming a Christian. He often refers to God's act of placing believers into Christ. In 1 Corinthians 12:13 he says, "By one Spirit we were all baptized into one body." This is why believers are called the Body of Christ. In 1 Corinthians 1:30 Paul says, "By [God's] doing you are in Christ Jesus." The Spirit of God has somehow baptized, or placed us, into Christ.

Theologians refer to this oneness with Christ as the "mystical union" of believers with Christ. Over one hundred times in the New Testament believers are said to be "in Christ," "in the beloved," "in Him," or similar phrases. The mystical union of the believer with Christ is not an obscure concept found off in the corner somewhere. Many of the most important promises God has given us are linked directly to this union. Here are some important examples:

TABLE 3.1 THINGS WE RECEIVE BASED ON OUR IDENTIFICATION WITH CHRIST

Passages	What Is Promised
Romans 8:1 There is therefore now no condemnation for those who are *in Christ Jesus*.	Freedom from condemnation
Romans 8:2 For the law of the Spirit of life *in Christ Jesus* has set you free from the law of sin and of death.	Freedom from the law of sin
Romans 8:39 [Neither] height. nor depth, nor any other created thing, shall be able to separate us from the love of God, which is *in Christ Jesus* our Lord.	Security and permanence in God's love
Romans 12:5 So we, who are many, are one body *in Christ*, and individually members one of another.	Unity with other Christians
1 Corinthians 1:30 But by His doing you are *in Christ Jesus,* who became to us wisdom from God, and righteousness and sanctification, and redemption.	God's wisdom, goodness, etc., imparted to us

Passages	What Is Promised
2 Corinthians 2:14 But thanks be to God, who always leads us in His triumph *in Christ*, and manifests through us the sweet aroma of the knowledge of Him in every place.	Triumph, or victory in spiritual war
2 Corinthians 5:17 Therefore if any man is *in Christ*, he is a new creature; the old things passed away; behold, new things have come.	New identity
Galatians 2:20 *I have been crucified with Christ*; and it is no longer I who live, but Christ lives in me; and the life which I now live in the flesh I live by faith in the Son of God, who loved me, and delivered Himself up for me.	Death to the old person
Galatians 3:28 There is neither Jew nor Greek, there is neither slave nor free man, there is neither male nor female; for you are all one *in Christ Jesus*.	Basis for social, racial, and sexual equality
Ephesians 1:3 Blessed be the God and Father of our Lord Jesus Christ, who has blessed us with every spiritual blessing in the heavenly places *in Christ*.	Every blessing; note the past tense
Philippians 3:9 [That I] may be found in Him, not having a righteousness of my own derived from the Law, but that which is through faith *in Christ*, the righteousness which comes from God on the basis of faith.	Righteousness imparted to us
Philippians 4:7 And the peace of God, which surpasses all comprehension, shall guard your hearts and your minds *in Christ Jesus*.	Inner peace of mind
Colossians 3:3-4 For you have died and your life is hidden with Christ in God. When Christ, who is our life, is revealed, then you also will be revealed with Him in glory.	Future inheritance and eternal life
1 John 5:20 And we know that the Son of God has come, and has given us understanding, in order that we might know Him who is true, and we are *in Him* who is true, *in His Son Jesus Christ*. This is the true God and eternal life.	Truth and understanding
2 Corinthians 5:21 He made Him who knew no sin to be sin on our behalf, that we might become the righteousness of God *in Him*.	The righteousness of God
1 Corinthians 1:5 In everything you were enriched *in Him*, in all speech and all knowledge.	Spiritual gifts

The overarching theme of the promises in these and other passages is that what is true of Christ has become true of we who are in Christ. Christ is victorious; therefore we are led in His victory. Christ is at the right hand of God; therefore we are also. According to Romans 6, death and resurrection are two of the most important things that are true of us if we are in Christ.

GOD'S VIEWPOINT

Whatever this teaching means, it must be very important, considering the promises attached directly to it. It may help to consider the problem from God's viewpoint.

As already stated, God's verdict on the Adam nature is final. We will never experience freedom from our fallen nature until we die and are resurrected in a new body. What is God to do in the meantime? One solution might be to strike dead immediately all who receive Christ and take them to Heaven right there and then. This solution has some obvious drawbacks. If everyone who believed in Christ immediately fell dead, Christian evangelism might become harder than it already is! Besides, who would do the witnessing?

Whether for this reason or others, this is not the direction God has decided to go. Instead of striking all believers dead, He has judicially *declared* them dead by identifying them with Christ. That is, He views us the same way He views His Son. This is certainly good news. Our standing before God couldn't be higher! But is it real? Or is this just double-talk? How can I be dead, risen, and seated in Heaven, when I am clearly sitting right here, seemingly the same as ever? A few points should help clarify this concept for us.

First, who views us as being "the righteousness of God"? I know I find it very hard to view myself that way. My wife finds it even harder! No, it is God who, in the first place, views me this way. But we should not take this to mean our identification with Christ is just some dream in the mind of God. Actually, our status is quite real. Consider the fact that one day our fallen existence will end, either when we die or when the Lord returns.

However, our standing in Christ will never end. When we think of it this way, our standing in Christ is even more "real" than our life in Adam.

Second, the fact that we have been identified with Christ is an item of faith for Christians. To cite 1 Corinthians 1:30 again: "By [God's] doing you are in Christ Jesus." That is a plain proposition that we might not fully understand, but we need to accept it as a direct declaration by God. We don't have to confirm this statement with some kind of experience or feeling. It is a fact of Scripture, which deserves willing belief from those of us who view Scripture as our ultimate standard of truth. The truest thing about us is what God says about us.

Remember, we did not sense or feel anything of Adam's fall, yet we received a fallen nature because he was our federal head. There certainly could be other explanations for why we have a selfish nature. The reason we, as Christians, believe our problems came from Adam is not because our experience tells us so, but because God has declared this to us in His Word.

God also declares that those of us who have trusted Christ have died and risen with Him, though we cannot feel this truth either. Therefore, we believe in our identification with Christ for the same reason that we believe in our identification with Adam—God tells us so.

Finally, when we consider our sense of identity, we realize that how God looks at us is not an unimportant abstraction. This idea is so important, and it comes up so often in the study to follow, that we will devote a whole chapter to understanding it.

IDENTITY: WHAT IS IT, AND HOW DO WE PERCEIVE IT?

When you look in the mirror, who looks back? Is it someone you know? Of course. "That's me!" you say. But more than this is involved in our total sense of identity. We also assign positive and negative values to ourselves. For instance, some of us might say, "That's me, the car dealer," or, "That's me, the musician." If we thought about it longer, we might add, "That's me, the wife of so-and-so," or, "That's me, the son of so-and-so." Then there would be some other value judgments: "That's me, the one with the big nose," or, "That's me, the fat one." With each element that comes to mind, we expand and complete our total sense of identity. Of course, many of us would include the observation, "That's me, the Christian."

Interestingly, not every feature of our bodies, life histories, or mental makeup would come to mind, even if we thought about it for a long time. Some things just don't figure into a consideration of who we are. For instance, we might never bother to point out, "That's me, the one with a filling in my twelve-year molar." It may well be that we have such a filling, and in that sense it is as much a part of the total description of who we are as the size of our nose. Yet, we may not view it as a significant part of our identity. Why not?

It is because we do not consider such a feature important. It may be real and measurable, but for some reason it just doesn't matter. The question is, why are some features considered important and therefore a part of the definition of our identity, while others aren't? The answer is that some things have been rendered important because of what other people say, and we draw our sense of identity from others' views of us.

> *We draw our sense of identity from others' view of us.*

A LONELY NIGHTMARE
Suppose nothing existed in the universe except you.

FIGURE 4.1

There you are, floating in a bubble in the midst of infinite, empty space. What would your identity be? What would you consider important? Suppose you asked yourself, "Am I tall or short?"

"Hmmm," you say. "Tall or short compared to whom?" Ideas like tall and short come from comparisons with others. But nothing and no one exists in this imaginary universe but you. Would you consider yourself smart or stupid? Here again, these concepts are directly dependent on perceptions of yourself *relative to others*. If you were the only one in the universe, such concepts would be meaningless. And so it would go in every area.

Whether it concerned things you did, features you found in yourself, or whatever, there would be no way to assign importance to these things. Consequently, you would have no sense of identity. You could only wonder who you were and whether you mattered, how you got there and where you were going; you could never know.

This nightmare is designed to illustrate a point. Your sense of identity, based on things about yourself that you consider important, is in turn based on others. That is: You have to be able to relate aspects of yourself to some reference point outside yourself.

> *You have to be able to relate aspects of your-self to some reference point outside yourself.*

ENTER EXTERNAL REFERENCE POINTS

Suppose in your lonely universe another person suddenly appears, also floating in a bubble.

FIGURE 4.2

At least now you have someone to compare yourself to. We could call this person an *external reference point*, because he or she isn't inside your head. You might notice you are taller than the other person and thus conclude that you are a tall person. However, for all you know, this other person might be the littlest midget ever, and you wouldn't be very tall, after all. Since both of you are floating in a sea of infinite nothingness, your comparisons would all be of questionable importance. You might notice that you have five fingers, but the other person in the universe has six. Is this important? Or just a curiosity? There is no way to tell.

You now have an external point of reference, a reference point outside yourself. The problem is, this external reference point is, like yourself, *finite*, or limited. There is no reason to think the other person's features are better or more authoritative than your own. Therefore, there is no way to tell what the real story is. Are you tall, or is the other person short? In such a universe, everything would be relative; nothing in the area of values would be certain.

Apart from God, the human race is living in this dilemma, and nontheistic thinkers are increasingly coming to realize it. Instead of one other person to compare ourselves with, according to secular thinkers, we have millions. This means we can begin to establish sociological averages, but nothing more.

You might find that, on average, you would be considered obese. This would be discouraging, especially if everyone around you thought fat people were ugly or bad. It is intriguing that in some poor countries today, being fat is a sign of wealth and is admired accordingly. Which perspective is right? Are fat people ugly? Or are they admirable and healthy looking? We might answer, "I'll decide for myself what I think about that." But probably the real truth is that we will answer according to the view of other people around us.

A WORLD ADRIFT

When we draw the camera back, we will realize that, although we as individuals are not floating alone in space without meaning, our whole planet is floating in space; so what's the difference? All the people on our planet decide somehow which comparisons are important and which are not. But if there is no absolute perspective to which we can relate our judgments, they are all quite arbitrary. In a real sense, such judgments are just as meaningless as the judgments we might arrive at when we were the only bubble.

Of course, this is not how we look at things. We begin as children, when our parents tell us what is important. They impart a lasting sense that some things about us are good and others are bad. They also teach us, often more by example than by words, what is important in general. We call this our value system.

Later in life, the opinions of our friends often come to have more importance than those of our parents. We may then modify part of the value system we received from our families. Generally, by the time we are adults, we have formed opinions about what matters and what doesn't, and we have formed some sense of our own identity. Yet, apart from God, we have no way of knowing whether any of these views are correct in any final way. For all we know (and in fact, it's a pretty good bet), we just happened to grow up around people who view things a certain way, and therefore we view things that way. It's no wonder many of us feel shaky about our sense of identity.

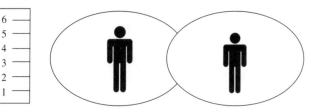

FIGURE 4.3

What if there were an absolute, or ultimate, ruler by which we could measure things? According to the biblical view, there is such an absolute. God is a reference point, but He is different from the finite reference point in our earlier illustration. Because He is infinite and unlimited, He is also universal, or absolute, rather than relative. Other things can be related to God, but He doesn't need to relate to anyone or anything to know who He is. With God as our reference point, we now have an *external, infinite reference point*. Such a reference point can tell us the way things are in the ultimate sense. No longer are things relative only to some other finite variable.

If we believe the Bible, we should realize that God's view of us is the true view, and that if He views us a certain way, then that is, in the ultimate sense, the way we really are! Even if the majority of our peers look at things differently, we could judge them incorrect by referring to the infinite external reference point—the God and Creator of all. Not only could we know that our peers' view is wrong in some cases, we could even find out that our *own view is wrong as well*. If we have come to view things a certain way, but God declares it's the other way, we need to change our mind.

MODERN SOLUTIONS

Modern thinkers are increasingly aware of the importance of what they like to call our "self-image." In the terminology we are using here, our self-image is our understanding of our identity, of who and what we are. These modern thinkers are referring to some of the same things the Apostle Paul spoke about in Romans 5 and 6, but their way of working with them is faulty. Modern teachers of self-image therapy urge us to shore up our shaky sense of identity in one of two ways. Neither is successful.

Some self-image theorists advocate pure, abstract self-affirmation. Like the comic figure in a current television series, you look in the mirror and say, "I'm smart enough, I'm good enough, and gosh darn it, people like me!" This satire is referring to an actual school of thinking seen in the massive flood of selfist literature filling bookshelves in our culture. You are supposed to repeat to yourself how good and valuable you are, in the belief that this will heal your sense of inadequacy and self-hate. But like the person in the bubble, there is no objective reason to believe any of these statements. The guy who says these things on the television series, for instance, tells himself he's okay, even though everyone can see he's a first-class nerd!

The concepts of "good" and "value" in themselves have no meaning without reference to a personal Creator God. We can tell ourselves anything we want, but if there is no reason to believe our statements are true, our words will have a hollow ring and the effect will be temporary at best.

Another direction taken by modern thinkers, including even Christian thinkers, is that the key to a good self-image lies in hanging around with people who will affirm us and tell us we are important. This solution is to be expected from secular thinkers, who base their understanding of personal identity and values on the views of others. It is quite odd, however, and even bizarre to hear such solutions from Christians.

The views and attitudes of others change regularly, and they often reflect falsehood. If we base our identity on what others think, we become the playthings of public opinion—we become man pleasers, dependent on others' views of us for our sense of well-being or identity.

> *Christians should know that we cannot base our identity on the views of other people.*

A DIFFERENT SOLUTION

If we study Scripture, we will find that this is not God's way. We Christians are not dependent on a vote by our affinity group to know who we are. We are not a group of bubbles floating in space, basing our understanding on comparisons with each other. We stand on the ground of the unchangeable character of God and His view of us.

This is why the Apostle Paul says in 2 Corinthians 10:12, "When [people] measure themselves by themselves, and compare themselves with themselves, they are without understanding." Paul understood what modern secular thinkers and even some modern Christian thinkers have not understood. Meaning and value are either determined by referring to God, our infinite, external reference point, or they are manufactured and changed at will by the shifting relative evaluations of the individual or the crowd.

We have seen that we need to know who we are and why we are important. The Bible answers these questions. According to God, when I was a nonChristian I was in Adam, and my identity was a certain way. Now I am in Christ, and I have a new identity. Now that we understand what personal identity is, we can return to the argument we were following in Romans.

KNOWING, BELIEVING, RECKONING

We left the book of Romans at the point where God said we who are "in Christ" have been united with Him in His death and resurrection from the dead. Our identity in Adam has ceased, and we now have a new identity. We are part of a new humanity in Christ. This language sounds terribly abstract and unreal when we first read it. Even some who have studied this passage for years still struggle with a sense that we are not fully experiencing the reality of this teaching. Rereading the passage may be of some help.

> Or do you not know that all of us who have been baptized into Christ Jesus have been baptized into His death? Therefore we have been buried with Him through baptism into death, in order that as Christ was raised from the dead through the glory of the Father, so we too might walk in newness of life. For if we have become united with Him in the likeness of His death, certainly we shall be also in the likeness of His resurrection, knowing this, that our old self was crucified with Him, that our body of sin might be done away with, that we should no longer be slaves to sin; for he who has died is

freed from sin. Now if we have died with Christ, we believe that we shall also live with Him, knowing that Christ, having been raised from the dead, is never to die again; death no longer is master over Him. For the death that He died, He died to sin, once for all; but the life that He lives, He lives to God. (Romans 6:3-10)

We have argued that the key to laying hold of this teaching for our daily lives is the issue of our identity. First, who am I? Then, how do I see myself? These two questions are not the same. It is possible for me to view myself as something different from what I actually am. In the area of self-image again, we disagree with modern secular teaching. To the secular thinker, the important thing is what I think of myself. If I think I'm cool, then I am. If I think I'm valuable, then I am. Whatever I think I am, that's what I am.

There is a truth here, but also an error. The error is that the secular view contains overtones of mind power common in New Age thinking. According to this doctrine, my mind supplies the power to shape reality. This is completely different from the biblical view.

According to the Bible, what matters is what I *actually am*. Only when I know the answer to this question can I exercise faith and use my mind to *experience* what I am. Under the New Age concept, it is my mind that shapes reality. Under the biblical model, it is reality, as defined by God, that my mind needs to understand and appropriate.

It is sadly possible to be one thing but to view ourselves as something different. We are subjective beings, so our view of ourselves may or may not be in accordance with reality. As we shall see, our faulty view of our identity may be interfering with our relationship with God. For instance, the fact that we have a new identity in Christ may be having little effect in our actual daily experience. This is sad, because in Christ's federal headship we have the basis for dealing with the problems we inherited from Adam—not a solution manufactured by our minds, but one that is actually true. The catch is that we have to first respond appropriately to our identification with Christ.

KNOWING

In Romans 6:1-10 the Apostle Paul refers several times to our *knowledge* of the facts regarding our mystical union with Christ. In verse 3 he says, "Or do you not know that all of us who have been baptized into Christ Jesus have been baptized into His death?" Again in verse 6 he says, "Knowing this. . . ." And finally, in verse 9 he says, "Knowing that. . . ." Three times in these few verses Paul seems to be calling us back to what we know, or should know, about our new identity in Christ. Knowing the facts is important. We cannot proceed further without accurately knowing the facts. Let's review the facts of Romans 6:1-10 before going on.

ONLY THE FACTS, PLEASE!

First, as we saw earlier, all Christians have been united with Christ through spiritual baptism. This is the act of God whereby He places us into the Body of Christ. He says "all of us" were baptized in this way, which means this unification with Christ is true of all Christians. It is not for the few or the elite. It is spoken of in the past completed tense, which means there is nothing any Christian needs to do to accomplish this unification. It is a historic fact.

This uniting with Christ means His death and resurrection also apply to us. We have served our death sentence under the Adam identity *vicariously*—through Christ. We have also risen with Christ, which means that, like Christ, we have access to a new, totally intimate relationship with God as His children. No longer need there be the separation between ourselves as sinners and the absolutely righteous Creator God. God views us as having the same standing as His own Son.

At the same time, my former master, sin, is no longer in charge. Christ is not only my closest friend, He is my new leader and authority. I now have the opportunity to follow Him instead of succumbing to slavery to my sin nature.

This is the way God views us. According to our findings in the last chapter, the way God views us is our true identity. This truth holds the key for victory in our lives.

AN IMPORTANT DISTINCTION

In verse 6, Paul says, "Knowing this, that our old self was crucified with Him, that our body of sin might be done away with, that we should no longer be slaves to sin." This statement can be misleading, unless we bear in mind the difference between our "old self," which was crucified with Christ, and our "body of sin." "Body of sin" refers to our sin nature, inherited from Adam, while "old self" refers to our identity in Adam. These two are not the same, even though they are related.

My old self is the person I was before receiving my new identity in Christ. That old self has been crucified. He no longer exists as far as God is concerned. This is why God says, "Therefore if any man is in Christ, he is a new creature; the old things passed away; behold, new things have come" (2 Corinthians 5:17). This is our new identity.

My body of sin, on the other hand, is the nature I also received from Adam. My sin nature is still there. It has not been "done away with" (Romans 6:6). This should be obvious. How could I think my sin nature has been done away with? Some sincere Christians have been wounded badly by this traditional translation of the verse, first found in the *King James Version*. Their conclusion, which is not unreasonable considering the translation, is that this verse is teaching perfectionism—the notion that we can become sinless in this life. But the Apostle John warns us, "If we say that we have not sinned, we make Him a liar, and His word is not in us" (1 John 1:10).

In truth, my sin nature is still alive. But if I respond correctly to the truth of my new identity in Christ, this sinful nature can be *rendered powerless*. This is how the Greek word *katargethe* should be translated. The *New American Standard Version* gives this reading in the margin as an alternative. I think it should be the preferred reading. Paul is trying to give us the key to breaking our sin nature's power over us. That key is a proper understanding and application of our new identity. We need not pretend we have no sin nature anymore. That solution would be closer to the notion of mind power we saw earlier: If I think I have no sin nature then perhaps I won't sin.

In this passage we are only being asked to recognize the truth. If we appropriate this truth, the awesome power of our sin nature can be broken to a substantial degree. God is not promising sinless perfection here; He is offering an opportunity for *relative* victory over sin.

BELIEVING
These are the facts: God doesn't look at us as being in Adam anymore, but in Christ. Do we believe this passage of Scripture? These statements are items of faith for Bible-believing Christians. Ask God to reveal the reality of these truths in your heart.

In a similar passage John says, "And we have come to know and have believed the love which God has for us" (1 John 4:16). Later, he is able to say, "We love, because He first loved us" (verse 19). We must come to know and to believe the truth about God's view of us before He will be free to change us accordingly.

RECKONING
Knowing the facts isn't enough. There is more we have to supply from our side before these facts move out of the abstract and into the practical.

Romans 6:11 says, "Even so consider yourselves to be dead to sin, but alive to God in Christ Jesus." In the *King James Version* it says we should "reckon" ourselves dead to sin but alive to God. Here is the first word of command in this passage. Until now, everything has already been accomplished for us by God. But here, He asks that we do something in response.

We already know how God views us. He sees us in Christ.

He views us as new creatures possessing the righteousness of God, as fellow heirs with Christ. But how do we view ourselves? Are we relating to God and others as new creatures, as people who have a new identity? Or are we relating as though we were in our old identity?

Let's reexamine this concept using the language in the following two verses:

> Therefore do not let sin reign in your mortal body that you should obey its lusts, and do not go on presenting the members of your body to sin as instruments of unrighteousness; but present yourselves to God as those alive from the dead, and your members as instruments of righteousness to God. (Romans 6:12-13)

Here, instead of saying "reckon yourselves such-and-so," Paul says, "present yourselves to God as such-and-so." But these are just two ways of saying the same thing.

We know what it means to present ourselves to God. This means we should pray, and in our heart we should offer ourselves to God as His followers. That much is easy. The interesting question is, Why does Paul add the phrase "as those alive from the dead"? What is the difference between offering ourselves to God normally, and offering ourselves to God as those alive from the dead?

If we can understand this difference we will have the key to applying the federal headship of Christ.

> *There is a huge difference between approaching God "in Adam" versus approaching Him "as those alive from the dead."*

THE GIGANTIC DIFFERENCE

The sad fact is, most of us usually approach God not as those alive from the dead, but as those in Adam! We come before God, often strongly conscious of sins we have committed and of our lack of faithfulness. Many of us actually cower before God, depressed about how unworthy we are to approach Him. After failing in the same area for the umpteenth time this week, it can be pretty difficult to saunter up to God and feel we have complete intimacy with Him.

Here the believer is being called on to exercise faith. It is easy to come before the Lord with thanksgiving and openness when we are in the flush of victory. But so much of the time we must approach Him in pain and failure. At such times, are we able to enter into His presence with ease and intimacy? If we are honest, we will probably have to admit that we often cannot. Why not? Because we are unable to see ourselves as He sees us.

COMING TO GOD IN ADAM

My son has trouble expressing himself when he has gotten into trouble or done poorly with his school work. Instead of sitting down with me for a good session of commiseration and exploration into the causes of the trouble, he usually is sullen and withdrawn. As his father, it hurts to try to talk to him and realize he feels ashamed to talk with me about it. He seems unable to find words much of the time and seems to want to cut the discussion short. He has even lied to avoid having me find out about a failure. He clearly has trouble realizing how I view him.

This must be similar to the way God feels when we skulk up to Him, reluctantly spending time in communion and wringing our hands fitfully the whole time.

When this is the case, we are presenting ourselves to God as those still in Adam, not as those alive from the dead. We are coming to God in our old identity rather than our new one. If we are honest, many of us will have to admit that this is the way we approach God most of the time.

It's no wonder God calls on us to consider (or reckon) ourselves dead to sin but alive to God in Christ Jesus. This tendency to view ourselves as though we were still in Adam is breaking down our intimacy with God and robbing the life from our Christian walks. We need to look much more closely at what it means to consider ourselves in our new identity.

CONSIDERING OURSELVES: THE SPECIFICS

The Apostle Paul exhorted the Roman Christians as follows: "Even so consider yourselves to be dead to sin, but alive to God in Christ Jesus" (Romans 6:11).

Some Bible teaching traditionally has stressed Paul's call in this passage to consider ourselves dead to sin. Believers are admonished to reckon themselves dead to sin each time temptation arises. Thus, it is argued, they will find deliverance . . . somehow or other. (The teaching gets vague at this point.)

As a young Christian I used to find this teaching rather confusing. If you have ever faced burning temptation by telling yourself, "I'm dead to this," you know what I mean. It doesn't work all that well, and I always felt I was trying to think my way into something that wasn't quite true. I sure didn't feel very dead!

But the verse doesn't say we should consider ourselves dead. We are obviously not dead. The real point of the verse is not just that we are dead to sin but that *we are alive to God!* We are to consider ourselves alive, not dead. We were alienated from God in Adam. Sin and death reigned over us. In Christ, we see ourselves *not* enslaved to sin, *not* alienated from God, but *alive* to God. We are treasured in His eyes. We are welcomed into the deepest level of intimacy with Him.

Only when we begin to consistently see ourselves this way and approach God this way will we experience the power of the victorious Christian life. Only then will we . . .

- ◆ begin to escape the performance fixation that leaves many believers defeated and broken in their own self-effort.
- ◆ realize the freedom and power of a perspective that is truly Christ-centered.
- ◆ gain regular, increasing freedom from our sin habits.
- ◆ be delivered to any extent from love demanding, self-pity, and selfish ingratitude.
- ◆ finally enter into authentic praise and worship of God.

How vital it is that we come to the place where, like Paul, we can say, "The life which I now live in the flesh I live by faith in the Son of God" (Galatians 2:20).

RELATING OUR RECKONING TO PROBLEMS WITH SIN

Verse 12 of Romans 6 ties together the notion of viewing ourselves in Christ with freedom from sin when it says, "Do not let sin reign in your mortal body." What is the relationship between these two?

In the first place, this passage is not teaching that anytime we have the right view of ourselves we will not sin, nor that it is impossible to sin while seeing ourselves in Christ. Rather than teaching the impossibility of sin, Paul is teaching the *incongruity* of sin as a way of life for those who are alive to God in Christ.

The relationship between freedom from sin and reckoning ourselves in Christ is not a mechanistic relationship. There is no formula we can repeat to ourselves when we feel tempted by sin that, once repeated, will stop the temptation (contrary to what some teachings on this passage almost seem to say). God is not giving us the magic words here, or a secret formula for battling the Devil per se. He is instead indicating how we should relate to Him and to ourselves on the basis of who we are.

In the longer view of our Christian walk over the course of years, those who operate this way will literally have more victory over sin in their lives. Those who fail to do so will automatically fall under the cloud of outward-oriented fakery, or they will just quit.

This alternative is spelled out for us in Romans 6:14—"For sin shall not be master over you, for you are not under law, but under grace."

The implication of this passage is all too clear. If we *were* under law, sin *would* be master over us! But why bring up law and grace in the context of how we consider ourselves? Because of the issue with which we began our study—doing versus being.

If we seek victory over sin purely from the perspective of what we are doing, we are functioning under law.[1] Under such a perspective, change is the result of altering our behavior. Changing what we do means we are changing what we are. This is a legal relationship. Under law, blessing depends on my performance.

Grace means that blessing has already been granted, and as we apprehend that fact, we will be transformed by it. Grace means that blessing does not depend on us to supply the power for change. Grace means that our behavior will change in a lasting, real way only as we change by the power of God. No wonder Paul teaches that only under grace can we experience freedom from sin. This truth flies in the face of those preachers and authors who beat the tambourine for righteous living from a motive of fear and threat! According to verse 14, such shrill warnings will only lead to further bondage to sin.

INDIRECT CHANGE

Let's consider the language in verse 13: "Do not go on presenting the members of your body to sin as instruments of unrighteousness; but present yourselves to God as those alive from the dead, and your members as instruments of righteousness to God."

We have already seen that the phrase "as those alive from the dead" is an essential qualifier. But what about the earlier phrase? Why does Paul say, "Do not go on presenting the members of your body to sin as instruments of unrighteousness"? Why not simply say, "Do not do unrighteous things"? It almost seems like Paul is not a clear writer. At the end of the verse there is a similar verbose phrase: "[Present] your members as instruments of righteousness to God." Here again, wouldn't it be easier to say, "Do righteousness" or "Do good"?

Paul was not an awkward writer. He carefully chose his phraseology to communicate a certain message and to avoid communicating the wrong message.

The message "do good," unless qualified, is Pharisaism. Such a statement focuses on outward performance in a way that, in this context, would be equivalent to presenting ourselves to God. In other words, such a formula would be defining our spirituality by our outward performance. But Paul's wording contains the cautious approach of one who understands the relationship between the believer's will and outward performance, or change. That relationship, in the larger picture, is an *indirect* one.

> *The relationship between our will and our outward performance is an indirect one.*

God does not call on believers to do good in this passage, but to present themselves to God, as it were, as instruments of goodness. This is because of our limited ability to change ourselves and our absolute need to depend on God for change. Rather than calling on believers to set their minds on law living, this verse calls on us to set our minds on God and on who we are in Christ. The result is a Christ focus rather than a sin focus!

To say that the relationship between character change and human will is indirect does not imply that we need not use our will. In fact, using our power of choice is essential. But we do not direct our will toward ourselves, ordering change of performance. We actively come forward to depend on God, who then uses His power to change us. We also must approach Him with the right perspective, which often entails a period of reflection and review. We might put it this way: We use our will to present ourselves to God with the right attitude and mind-set, and God then uses His power to change us.

> *We use our will to present ourselves to God with the right attitude and mind-set, and God then uses His power to change us.*

As we live this lifestyle over a period of time (usually years), we will discover gradual change in our characters. Indirectly, we have used our will, and change has occurred as the Holy Spirit empowers us for it.

The difference between these two understandings is immense, even though we may easily become confused about which view we are adopting at a given moment. Ironically, we can realize repeatedly that we have arrogantly sought to bypass God in our quest for good works, even though we may understand the theory behind this passage perfectly.

"BEING" APPLIED TO "DOING"

In Romans 6:17-19 we have a restatement of this principle in very clear terms:

> But thanks be to God that though you were slaves of sin, you became obedient from the heart to that form of teaching to which you were committed, and having been freed from sin, you became slaves of righteousness. I am speaking in human terms because of the weakness of your flesh. For just as you presented your members as slaves to impurity and to lawlessness, resulting in further lawlessness, so now present your members as slaves to righteousness, resulting in sanctification.

The following diagram may help us understand this language. Paul first refers to the Romans' past conversion.

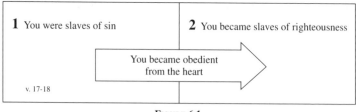

FIGURE 6.1

This is a simple statement of what has already occurred. Our identity as slaves of sin in Adam has been altered to a new identity—that of slaves of righteousness in Christ. Now comes an imperative, a word of command, based on that past fact.

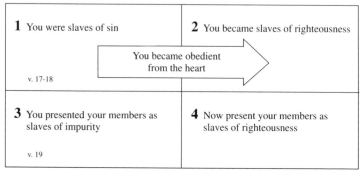

FIGURE 6.2

In this diagram, we have added two frames below to represent verse 19. God is saying, "When you *were* slaves of sin, you presented yourselves as slaves of impurity" (the left column of boxes). Nothing could be more reasonable than that! How else would slaves of sin present themselves? When unconverted, we acted as what we were: sinners. Our intent and focus was not on how to avoid sin or how to do righteousness, but on how to enjoy sin and preserve our freedom to sin.

Now we have moved from box 1 to box 2. What should be the result? Obviously, we should now adopt the focus of one who is a slave of righteousness and present ourselves accordingly. Paul uses the words *members* or *members of your bodies* in this section to mean "yourself in this life," or, as we will cover later, your *condition*. Careful reading will show that it is not just our physical bodies, but our whole selves in this life, that we are to present to God.

But this is not always the case. It is sadly possible to move from box 1 to box 2 but not from box 3 to box 4. When this is the case, we are basing our lives on our old identity. We are failing to acknowledge or to present ourselves in our new identity. An illustration may help us understand this concept.

Suppose I have a friend who is a criminal. He is sentenced to twenty years in prison for various crimes and serves the time in one of the harshest dungeons ever built. In his stone cell he learns to scratch lines on the wall to keep track of the days, and he even has to use a bucket in the corner as his toilet.

Finally, after twenty years, I pick him up on the day he is freed. I insist he come to my house and occupy the guest room while he adjusts to freedom. But things don't progress as expected. I find he rarely leaves his room, and before long I notice a smell coming from the room. Finally, I stop by and ask to come in. As he lets me into the room I am horrified to see that he has been scratching lines on my freshly painted wall, and he has soiled my wastebasket!

What would you say if he were your friend? I know what I'd say: "Hey, pal, haven't you overlooked something? You're not in prison anymore!" I would say the same thing Paul is saying in this passage. "You used to do these things when you were a prisoner because you had no alternative. You can *still* do them— it's *possible* to do them—even though you're now free. But how incongruous! How unbefitting! Now that you're free, why don't you begin to live as a free person?"

I could get heavy with him, threatening him with expulsion from the house, but this would be off-target. I want him to stop his antisocial behavior, especially the bit with the trash can! But it's clear this person doesn't realize his freedom. It would be a shame if he changed his behaviors because I threatened him, without ever realizing the reason and basis for change.

God wants us to understand what He has done to our identity. He wants us to experience this change increasingly in our lives, not through gritting our teeth in self-effort but through the power of His transforming love.

UNDERSTANDING THE PROPOSITION

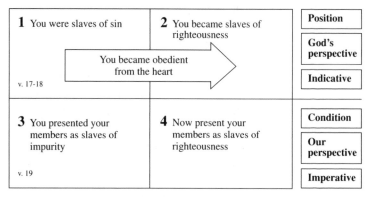

FIGURE 6.3

POSITION VERSUS CONDITION

In this version of our diagram, we have filled in some terminology on the right side that will help us understand the relationships between the boxes. The first words in the groups above and below the center line are *Position* and *Condition*. These words have been used by Bible teachers to describe the difference between what is judicially true of us and what is true of us in our experience. Our *position* refers to the way God looks at us and is based on the past work of Christ and our identification with Him. Our daily successes and failures play no part in our standing, or position, before God. Our position before God is unchangeable for all eternity.

Our *condition* refers to our daily experience, which can rise and fall through well-being and adversity, spiritual health

and sickness. One day our condition may be that we are presenting ourselves to God as those alive from the dead, while
another day we may be fleeing from God. One day we feel
victorious; the next we feel defeated. These changes depend
on circumstances and on how we are responding to them and
to the truths about ourselves. We hope to see improvement in
our condition (the process of sanctification), but this will take
time.

GOD'S PERSPECTIVE VERSUS OUR PERSPECTIVE
The next set of boxes above and below the center line in the
diagram (page 52) contain the words *God's perspective* and *Our
perspective*. These terms refer to the fact that God always views
us in our position. We, on the other hand, are prone to view ourselves in our condition. The things that are real to us are not the
truths of the Word of God but our experiences, our circumstances, and our feelings. At times it is strikingly obvious that
the truth of our position in Christ means little to us. The almost
complete lack of gratitude in our hearts so much of the time
betrays the fact that we see ourselves in our condition, not in
our position. Our prayers reflect this conditional focus. We fret
and whine about our experiences, our circumstances, and our
feelings. We often have little or nothing to say to God about our
position in Christ.

Here is the real lesson of this passage. God wants us to begin
viewing ourselves the way He views us, to adopt His point of
view about ourselves and even about others. God has included
this passage and many others like it in the New Testament
because He thinks it is important that we see ourselves in our
position, not just in our condition. The New Testament would not
have devoted so much space to this discussion if it were not
central in importance.

INDICATIVE VERSUS IMPERATIVE
The final pair of terms in the diagram are *Indicative* and *Imperative*. These are terms from grammar. By using the appropriate

grammar, we can either say how things *are* or how they *should be*. When we describe the way things are, we are using the *indicative* mood. When we say how things should be, like when we issue a command, we are using the *imperative* mood.

When Scripture teaches, "By God's doing you are in Christ Jesus," it is making an indicative statement. It tells us the way things already are. When God says, "Therefore, reckon yourselves dead to sin but alive to God in Christ Jesus," He is making an imperative statement, a statement of command. He is telling us what we are supposed to do.

It should be obvious that Scripture contains both indicative and imperative statements. This is nothing new, although some schools of theology seem to be embarrassed by imperatives in the Bible. God *does* command, and we need to include that fact in our theology. Numerous books have come out recently that make the reader wonder what their authors think about the imperatives of Scripture. Modern man is repulsed by the authority of God, but God still thinks His authority is good.

However, there is more to see here. We need to see the *relationship* between the indicative and the imperative statements in the Bible. We notice a pattern in this passage in Romans 5 and 6, as well as in the rest of the New Testament. Namely, the imperatives, or commands, given to us in Scripture are *consistently* dependent on the indicative statements describing what God has done. Stated differently, What we are supposed to do is always based on what God has already done.[2]

> *What we are supposed to do is always based on what God has already done.*

This may sound like a lot of theological mumbo jumbo, but it is vitally important for every Christian. The relationship between the indicative (what God has done or is going to do) and the imperative (what I am supposed to do) goes to the heart of two important components of our motives.

In the first place, because God's instructions are based on what He has already done, I obey, not *in order* to gain my standing with God but *because* I have a right standing with God. The difference here is profound. We can explain it with two questions: Am I trying to give God a reason to bless me? Or am I responding to the fact that He already has blessed me?

◆ If I answer "yes" to the first question, I am functioning under law. My blessing and my standing with God depend on my performance for Him. But Romans 6 just said we are no longer under law! We will study this more in the next chapter.

◆ If I answer "yes" to the second question, I am properly motivated. I am not trying to earn anything. I realize who I am. Unlike my prisoner friend, I realize I am no longer a prisoner, and I am responding accordingly. It is quite fascinating and liberating to see this relationship unfold

> *Am I trying to give God a reason to bless me? Or am I responding to the fact that He already has blessed me?*

in one passage after another throughout the New Testament. A few choice examples are included in the Appendix.

Seeing the imperative as depending on the indicative is what separates the pharisaical Christian from what we might call the *resting* Christian. A resting Christian is one who depends on the power of God for character change, and who is secure in his or her acceptance during the process. Some teaching today puts so much emphasis on the imperatives of Scripture that virtually all the importance of scriptural indicatives seems lost. When we constantly bang away at the imperatives of Scripture without carefully covering and reviewing the *basis* for such commands (the gracious gifts of God), we create a grotesque caricature of the true God, even though we may be able to quote isolated verses to support our position. The relationship between the indicatives and the imperatives becomes confused or even reversed under such teaching.

Suppose your dad gave you a brand-new car for your birthday. As he hands you the keys he says, "There are two things I want you to know about this car. The first is that it is a free gift from me to you. The second is that it's going to cost you ten thousand dollars." Obviously, the first statement is rendered incomprehensible because the second statement cancels it out. Ownership of the car is apparently conditional. What if I refuse to pay the ten thousand dollars? It seems that ownership of the car itself will be removed. Likewise, when law-oriented teachers bang away at imperatives endlessly, we forget what the indicatives mean and why they are important.

What if your father took a different approach? Suppose as he handed you the keys he said, "This car is a free gift from me to you, and because of that, I hope you will respond to such a generous gift by using it responsibly." This is an entirely different model from the first example, and it is more like what God is handing us in this passage. Ownership of the car does not depend on our using it responsibly. On the contrary! Our responsible use of the car depends on our ownership of it. It is *because* we have been given a generous gift that we are being asked to do something.

GIVE ME THE BIG PICTURE ONE LAST TIME

In your hands you hold this book. Suppose the book could speak to you, and it said this: "I know I have fallen short. I want to change but I don't feel able. I know what I need to be, but I am not. Please give me the ability . . . give me the grace and the power to become . . . a book!"

I know what I would say. I'd say, "Now wait a minute. Hold it right there. You already are a book!" This surreal and, I admit, bizarre illustration must be similar to what God feels when we completely ignore our identity in Christ and insist on relating to Him as though we were in Adam.

Let's consider it a different way. How much effort do you expend trying to avoid wetting your pants or shaking a rattle? I know I don't spend any energy at all trying to avoid these things. They are activities I used to do, and I probably even enjoyed doing them. But these days, I have no particular urge to engage in this kind of activity. I did those things when I was a baby. Now, it just wouldn't be appropriate, because I'm an adult. I *could* still do these things. It is certainly possible. But it would be incongruous and ridiculous.

There may have even been a transition period when I struggled to change my ways. My parents might have said, "Act your age!" But eventually, I accepted that I wasn't a baby anymore, and I turned away from such activities for good. We might say that when I turn away from these infantile behaviors, I am acting out of what I am—an adult. For that reason, it causes little or no strain for me to behave this way.

Unfortunately, changing in the moral area won't be as easy as learning to go to the bathroom. Learning to change in nonmoral ways is easy. There is nothing in my nature that insists on wetting my pants. Changing from autonomy to God-centered submission will grate on me quite a bit more, but the principle for change will be similar.

What terrible frustration and confusion we would feel if we tried to enter a room we were already in! It's no different when we struggle to become someone we already are. The key for many of us is to begin turning away from who we were in Adam and accept who we are in Christ. We need to begin to consider ourselves dead to sin and alive to God in Christ Jesus.

It is wonderful to realize God has acted on my behalf—independently, irrevocably, and lovingly. He has given me a new identity in Christ. When this indicative, what the author of Hebrews calls this "finished work," breaks in on me fully, my relationship with God will be revolutionized. In place of the moan of defeat forming on my lips will spring words and songs of praise.

NOTES

1. Theologians often use the term *legalism* to refer to the doctrine that people are justified, or saved, by works. *Nomism*, on the other hand, refers to those who believe they are saved by grace but must live the Christian life by law. In this study, we use the terms *under law* and *legalism* to mean nomism, not technical legalism. This is in accord with the popular use of the words, and this is a popular study.

2. We have focused on the past tense indicative here, but indicatives also apply to the present or the future. For instance, God says He will give us an inheritance in eternity future. This is an indicative statement that serves as a basis for numerous imperative statements, such as those urging us to "lay up for [ourselves] treasures in heaven" (Matthew 6:20).

LAW SCHOOL

The notion of acting on the basis of who we are in Christ is such a beautiful concept, but somehow it just isn't complete. As you read the previous chapter, you may have been clucking your tongue and shaking your head. "It isn't that easy," you say. "I've heard something like this before, but it doesn't work."

Too often, we will find that our efforts to reckon ourselves alive to God in Christ seem to make little difference, especially in the short run. We must emphasize again that this is not a magic state of mind that will preclude failure. This mind-set is the *backdrop* for the dramatic but gradual measures God will take in our spiritual growth. With an inherited nature tending toward sin and autonomy, as well as years and even decades of trusting that nature to run our lives, fundamental change won't come easily. Part of that process will surely be numerous painful lessons in what might be called *law school*. Law school is the subject of the next chapter (7) in Romans.

A RADICAL, EXTREMIST PASSAGE

Romans 7:1-6 is one of the most extreme and startling passages in the Bible. Why not read it carefully right now?

Or do you not know, brethren (for I am speaking to
those who know the law), that the law has jurisdiction
over a person as long as he lives? For the married
woman is bound by law to her husband while he is living; but if her husband dies, she is released from the law
concerning the husband. So then if, while her husband is
living, she is joined to another man, she shall be called
an adulteress; but if her husband dies, she is free from
the law, so that she is not an adulteress, though she is
joined to another man. Therefore, my brethren, you also
were made to die to the Law through the body of Christ,
that you might be joined to another, to Him who was
raised from the dead, that we might bear fruit for God.
For while we were in the flesh, the sinful passions,
which were aroused by the Law, were at work in the
members of our body to bear fruit for death. But now we
have been released from the Law, having died to that by
which we were bound, so that we serve in newness of
the Spirit and not in oldness of the letter.

Divorce laws have changed a lot since the Apostle Paul's
day, but the legal principle he is discussing has not. The law
only has jurisdiction over someone while that person is alive.
As in most analogies, inconsistencies arise if we press it too far.
For instance, the woman in this passage apparently refers to us.
We are bound to a demanding husband who is impossible to
please—the Law of God. To be perfectly consistent, the husband should die before the woman is free. But that would mean
the Law of God dies, which is not possible. So, the one who
dies in the analogy is actually the woman herself—that is, us.

Death severs the bonds of law. Because we have died with
Christ, we have moved beyond the reach of the law. Death sev-
ers the bonds of our civil law today just as it does the Law of
God—the Old Testament Law brought down from Mount Sinai.
The Law only has jurisdiction over us while we live. Since God
views us as having died with Christ, where does this leave us

with regard to the Law of God? Paul clearly gives us our answer in verse 6: The law no longer has jurisdiction over us!

Some Christians will cough and sputter, as this naked truth offends their senses. A tightening in the throat may already be compelling some to reach for concordances and commentaries, to find passages that show why this text shouldn't be taken too

> *The law no longer has jurisdiction over us!*

literally. Within minutes, those offended will be able to relax again, secure in the knowledge that the wheels aren't coming off and that, if we understand the background material, we are under law, after all—this passage applies to someone or something else. It surely doesn't mean the Law of God has no jurisdiction over me!

But let's hold on for a minute and give this section of inspired Scripture a chance. We can go to our resources later if we still feel the need. For right now, we should ask ourselves, "Why does God say, 'Therefore, my brethren, you also were made to die to the Law'? Why does He say, 'But now we have been released from the Law, having died to that by which we were bound, so that we serve in newness of the Spirit and not in oldness of the letter'?" (verse 6).

What does it mean to serve in the "newness of the Spirit and not in oldness of the letter"? What is the "letter" we do *not* serve in? As we take up the answers to these questions, we might as well also examine a similar parallel passage in 2 Corinthians 3 that uses language almost identical to that in Romans 7:

> Our adequacy is from God, who also made us adequate as servants of a new covenant, not of the letter, but of the Spirit; for the letter kills, but the Spirit gives life. But if the ministry of death, in letters engraved on stones, came with glory, so that the sons of Israel could not look intently at the face of Moses because of the glory of his face, fading as it was, how shall the ministry of the Spirit fail to be even more with glory? (2 Corinthians 3:5-8)

The legal code Moses brought down from the mountain is called the "ministry of death" here, and Paul says we do not serve that covenant.

The questions raised by these and similar passages in the New Testament are vital for growing Christians. Both of the above sound like outright repudiations of the Law as the governing authority over Christians. But a number of explanations have been advanced to explain why these passages don't mean what they seem to be saying.

OTHER ALTERNATIVES:
"NO MORE UNDER LAW FOR SALVATION"
Some interpreters argue, "These passages just say we are not under the law for *salvation*, but of course we *are* under the Law of God when it comes to spiritual growth. Only nonChristians are under law in the ultimate sense." This is true in the sense that they are ultimately accountable to either keep the whole law or answer to the justice of God. But, as we shall see, Paul also says Christians are no longer under the law for spiritual growth.

Paul is not just discussing the terms for salvation in these passages. He is also discussing spiritual growth and Christian living. This must be true, or what would be the difference between the "new covenant" and the "old covenant" as mentioned in the 2 Corinthians passage? Not even under the Old Covenant were people saved by obeying the law. Romans 4:1-8 makes this clear, as do many other passages. Old Testament saints were not saved by works, and this is not really disputed by anyone involved in the debate over Romans 7. Old Testament saints were also saved by grace. So, if neither Old Testament nor New Testament saints are saved by works, what is the difference between the New Covenant, which is said to be "not of the letter" (that is, not of the law), and the Old Covenant?

The difference is that those who serve under the New Covenant are no more under law when it comes to spiritual growth. It is *growth*, not birth, that is in view here. People have never been born anew by law. The amazing truth is that the law has no jurisdiction over Christian believers. God means it when He says, "We have been released from the law."

OTHER ALTERNATIVES:
"NO MORE UNDER CEREMONIAL OR CIVIL LAW"

Some interpreters will take a different direction. They argue that it is the ceremonial and perhaps even the civil laws of the Old Testament that we are "no longer under." The moral laws, on the other hand, must always be binding. After all, didn't Jesus warn against setting aside the laws of God? In Matthew 5:19 He said, "Whoever then annuls one of the least of these commandments, and so teaches others, shall be called least in the kingdom of heaven; but whoever keeps and teaches them, he shall be called great in the kingdom of heaven." These interpreters would argue that the only way to harmonize Jesus' statement with Paul's is to see Paul as referring to the ceremonial law, while Jesus is referring to the unchangeable moral law of God.

This argument sounds plausible, but it won't fit the language or the context of the passages we are studying. It also fails to harmonize the passages.

In Romans 7, Paul gives an example of how law doesn't work when it comes to spiritual growth. In verses 7 and 8 he cites a law—"You shall not covet"—as an example of this principle. This is no ceremonial law! This is a moral law.

Again in 2 Corinthians 3, Paul says we serve under "a new covenant, not of the letter, but of the Spirit; for the letter kills, but the Spirit gives life." This letter that "kills," what is it? In the context, Paul explains that the letter that kills is the "ministry of death, in letters engraved on stones." This could only be referring to the Ten Commandments. The Ten Commandments are not ceremonial laws. They are moral laws (except for the Sabbath law). If we were still under the moral law, why

> *We are not under law for spiritual growth.*

would Paul say we do not serve under this letter? Why does he say this letter, the moral law of God, kills, but the Spirit gives life? He says this because Christians are not under the moral law any more than they are under the ceremonial law.

For those interested in exploring this question further, we have summarized the main arguments advanced against the notion that Christians are not under law with a short response to each in the following chart.

TABLE 7.1 THE "UNDER LAW" DEBATE: WHAT DOES PAUL MEAN BY THIS PHRASE?

Arguments that We Must Remain Under Law as a Rule of Life	Responses Showing We Are Not Under Law as a Rule of Life
We are "not under law" means we are not justified, or saved, by law.	No one was ever saved by law, so if this were true, the New Covenant wouldn't be anything new after all (Galatians 2:16).
We are "not under law" means we are no longer under the ceremonial law (sacrificial system); we are still under the moral law of God.	The example Paul cites in Romans 7:7 is the Tenth Commandment. It is a moral law. Also, the "ministry of death, in letters engraved on stones" (2 Corinthians 3:7) does not refer to ceremonial laws, but to the Ten Commandments, which are mostly moral laws.
In Romans 8:9 Paul says, "You are not in the flesh but in the Spirit, if indeed the Spirit of God dwells in you. But if anyone does not have the Spirit of Christ, he does not belong to Him." Therefore, Paul is comparing Christians with nonChristians when he speaks of those who walk by the Spirit and those who are according to the flesh, as he also does in 7:5.	Paul does use the phrases "in the flesh" and "in the Spirit" to refer to Christians versus nonChristians. However, he also uses another phrase, "*according* to the flesh or Spirit" (emphasis added), which refers to carnal versus spiritually minded Christians. Contrast Romans 8:4-7 with 8:8-9 (see also Galatians 5:18). We will study this passage in detail later in this book.
Paul says he "was once alive apart from the Law" because Hebrew boys were not responsible to keep the Law until their bar mitzvah at age thirteen.	It is highly unlikely that Paul would ever say he was alive apart from the law as a nonChristian. This goes against his doctrine of spiritual death before regeneration in Christ (see Romans 5:18, Ephesians 2:1). It is better to understand this as referring to a period early in his Christian life.

Arguments that We Must Remain Under Law as a Rule of Life	Responses Showing We Are Not Under Law as a Rule of Life
How can we not be under the Law of God, when God's character never changes?	God's character can be reflected in the law without us being "under" it. The problem is not with the law, but with our rebellious reaction to the law, which renders it ineffective as a tool for life change.
Jesus taught that He did not come to abolish the law. He also warned that "Whoever then annuls one of the least of these commandments, and so teaches others, shall be called least in the kingdom of heaven; but whoever keeps and teaches them, he shall be called great in the kingdom of heaven" (Matthew 5:19).	Jesus taught that He "did not come to abolish the law, *but to fulfill it*" (Matthew 5:17, emphasis added). This means either that the law is a term for the Old Testament, which He fulfilled, or that Christ fulfilled the legal requirements of the law on our behalf. Jesus spoke in the period before His own death. This is why Paul said Jesus was "born of a woman, born under the Law" (Galatians 4:4). During this period, the New Covenant of the Spirit was not available, because "the Spirit was not yet given" (John 7:38-39). The Sermon on the Mount ministers to those who were trying to bring the law down to the level where it could be kept by human effort. Jesus stressed the absolute demands of the law for those who mistakenly believed they could be justified by works.
Although the context of Romans 7 is spiritual growth (see Romans 6), the truths about our spiritual birth give us our basis for growth. This is why Paul returns to a consideration of the dynamics of conversion in Romans 7 (for instance, verse 5).	The context for Romans 7 is indeed Romans 6, which discusses spiritual growth (verses 11-19), and Romans 8, which also discusses growth. However, while these passages mention conversion, the pattern of argument is always the same. Namely, Paul points out that we should remember our conversion, and our growth should proceed in accordance with that new identity. Since interpreting in light of the context is the first rule of Bible interpretation, we should prefer to understand Romans 7 as referring to growth also.

To summarize, neither of the "under law" explanations adequately answers the questions raised in these passages. Instead, we are driven to the conclusion that Christians have been released from the law, just as it seems to be saying in Romans 7.

Those who believe Christians are still under the law for growth have raised some good questions. "How can we be released from the Law of God?" "Has God's moral character changed?" To understand the answers to such questions, we need a comprehensive understanding of God's reasons for giving the law. Only then will we be able to view the law correctly while avoiding legalism.

WHY THE LAW? DEFINING SIN

Surely right is right, and wrong is wrong, for Christians just as for everyone else? Yes, and the Law does have a legitimate role to play in defining sin. The principles underlying the Old Testament Law still define good and evil, as they always have. But the believer under grace looks at the law, not for detailed instructions for living, but for a general picture of God's character.

A good example of principled application of the law is Paul's statement that the whole Law is summed up in the saying "You shall love your neighbor as yourself" (Romans 13:9). This is a nonlegalistic analysis. No legalist would feel comfortable with a statement like this. It is too general, and it leaves too much freedom. Even though details are included, like not committing adultery and not stealing, it still leaves far too much to the imagination. As we shall see, details are important for legalists. Paul refers to this defining role of the law in Romans 7:7—

> What shall we say then? Is the Law sin? May it never be! On the contrary, I would not have come to know sin except through the Law; for I would not have known about coveting if the Law had not said, "You shall not covet."

Although as a nonChristian I might have felt that lusting was all right, once I confronted the Bible, I realized it was wrong. But what am I to do with that knowledge now that I have it? This is what separates the legalist from the nonlegalist. The legalistic approach is to find the appropriate law for a given situation and apply it strictly.

The grace-oriented Christian approaches right and wrong in a completely different way. Under the covenant of the Spirit, we look beneath the law to learn the great ethical principles underlying the case laws in the Bible. Then we look to the leading of the Spirit and the expediency of the moment to determine how to react in a given situation in harmony with those principles.

A good example of this flexible, or principled, use of the law is Paul's teaching on eating things sacrificed to idols in 1 Corinthians 8 and 10 as well as Romans 14. Paul never says whether it is right or wrong to eat this meat, but he seems to argue that it could be different for different people and even different in different situations. He even goes so far as to suggest that if someone served meat to a Christian guest, the guest should simply not ask whether it was sacrificed to idols. Only if the server offers this information should the Christian react by refusing to eat it. Legalistic thinkers are troubled and confused by such a teaching. Is it right or wrong to eat this meat? That depends. The believer operating under grace realizes that our knowledge of right and wrong is not to be governed by a legal code, but by ethical principles embodied therein, especially love.

We see a similar example in 1 Corinthians 7:17-24. There Paul argues that we should stay in the condition in which we were called. "Grow where you were planted" seems to be the crux of his argument. Then he goes on to detail several applications of the principle. But surprisingly, he suddenly begins to throw in exceptions. Slaves should go ahead and get their freedom. Virgins can marry if they really want to (verses 25-28). This is not a law, it is a flexible ethical principle that might not apply in certain situations. This is not legalistic thinking.

The ability to deal with moral principles without falling "under law" comes to those who view the law in a nonlegalistic way. It is not that the law is no longer there, but that I am no longer *under* it. Focusing on a list of rules, or orienting my thinking around rules, will not help me live the Christian life. As we shall see, God wants my attention directed to Him, not to the law or to my failure to keep the law.

When I look in my mirror these days, it shows me that I am beginning to sag in the middle. But while my mirror can show me my problem, it does nothing to help me change it. I can poke, twist, and pose, but the sagging gut is still there. The mirror is not designed to do anything about that. Likewise, the law lets me know where I am falling short, but it can do nothing to help me change.

The law shows us right and wrong, and in so doing, it reveals our problem. We fall short. Just as the law convicts the nonChristian of sin, it shows us as Christians that we still need ongoing grace from God. But here is a strange thing. The law not only shows us we are committing sin, it also provokes us to sin *more*.

WHY THE LAW? PROVOKING SIN

NonChristians are actually provoked to sin by the reaction of their flesh nature to God's law, as Paul said in Romans 7:5— "While we were in the flesh, the sinful passions, which were aroused by the Law, were at work in the members of our body to bear fruit for death."

A story is told of a new hotel built overhanging the Gulf of Mexico. The second-floor balcony hung over the gulf in a way that made the management think people might try to fish from the balcony. The management was afraid of liability problems, and they thought the heavy fishing weights might break the expensive picture windows behind the fishermen. They decided just before opening week to post signs in each room forbidding fishing from the balcony.

During the opening week, several windows were damaged

by fishing gear. At an employee meeting, they discussed further sanctions. Should they fine those who fished? Should they turn them out of the hotel? A wise employee suggested that before enacting draconian measures, they should try taking the signs down. They did, and they never had another incident!

In verse 8 of Romans 7 Paul describes this effect of the Law: "But sin, taking opportunity through the commandment, produced in me coveting of every kind; for apart from the Law sin is dead."

What a strange saying, and how difficult it is to fit it into some modern theology! According to this verse, the law does more than just define sin. It stimulates the sin nature and produces more sin, even in Christians. He goes so far as to say that "apart from the Law sin is dead." This statement implies that coming out from under law is part of the key to breaking the power of sin in our lives. How similar this statement is to Romans 6:14, cited earlier: "For sin shall not be master over you, for you are not under law, but under grace."

In both statements the implication is the opposite of what modern legalistic teachers would have us believe. Far from suggesting that the Law might help us live for God, these verses seem to be saying that the Law encourages rebellion and sin. Notice yet another passage supporting this notion, 1 Corinthians 15:56, which says, "The sting of death is sin, and the power of sin is the law." One of the most startling verses on this is Romans 5:20—"And the Law came in that the transgression might increase; but where sin increased, grace abounded all the more." Does it seem strange that the law was designed to *increase* sin? We would normally think the law was there to decrease sin! But this says the opposite!

YOU'VE GOT TO BE KIDDING!

Why would God want to give a law that stimulates sin? Certainly, He is not pleased by humans committing sin. But for some reason, according to these passages, He has provided a law that He knew would stimulate sin.

We have all experienced this truth. Isn't the forbidden fruit more exciting? We have probably seen this tendency in our children, because they don't know enough to hide it yet. All we need to do is suggest that maybe our two-year-old son shouldn't climb that ledge, and there he goes!

But what does God get out of this? You can probably guess the answer. God did not give the Law because He thought it would be obeyed. Neither did He need a mirror with which to see our sin. God already knows all about our sin. *We* are the ones who are confused. *We* are the ones who need the Law to serve as a "tutor to lead us to Christ" (Galatians 3:24). The Law convinces us that nothing less than the free gift of God will save us.

But what about Christians? What point would there be in having a law to stimulate Christians' sin natures? Essentially, the purpose is the same. Although we now realize we cannot save ourselves by good works, we may secretly believe we are able to follow God in our own strength. Even if we say, "Yes, I know I'm unable to change myself," God may detect a lingering confidence in self. He will "smoke out" this confidence by allowing us to tangle with His Law just as Paul does in Romans 7:14-24.

HOW DOES IT WORK?
As Christians, some of us tiptoe over the line in smaller ways, but we are all still thrilled on some level by violating the law. That's what our fallen nature is like! That nature is not gone just because we have a new standing in Christ. However, if we understand our new identity, we can rob the sin nature of its awesome power over us. And part of understanding our new identity is realizing we are no longer under law. In verses 9-11 of Romans 7 Paul says,

> I was once alive apart from the Law; but when the commandment came, sin became alive, and I died; and this commandment, which was to result in life, proved to

result in death for me; for sin, taking opportunity
through the commandment, deceived me, and through it
killed me.

This statement refers to an experience Paul had as a
Christian. Certainly, he would never suggest that he was "alive"
at one time before his conversion, no more than he would claim
he was not under law before conversion. On the contrary, this
time when he was "alive apart from the Law" refers to that
period *after* conversion when he felt the joy of the Lord intensely,
though he had not truly matured.

IS THIS A CHRISTIAN?

Let's linger for a moment on the question of whether this passage is describing a Christian or nonChristian experience. This
question is important, because when interpreters argue that it is
referring to a nonChristian experience, they also conclude that
while nonChristians are not under law for salvation, Christians
may indeed be under law as a rule of life. Therefore, a great
deal hinges on this question.

Some wonder how, if being alive is only possible for a
Christian, Paul can say he later died. If only a Christian can
be called "alive," shouldn't only a nonChristian be called
"dead"? The answer is that while a Christian could be called
"dead," a nonChristian could never be called "alive." We already
argued in chapter 6 that it is possible to go from death to life
in our position, but not in our condition. Therefore, the best
way to understand this passage is that it is referring to a
Christian experience.

We reach the same conclusion for at least two other reasons. First, later in Romans 7, as Paul describes the struggle
under law, he refers to the "inner man" (verse 22) that joyfully
concurs with the Law of God and the "members of my body"
(verse 23) that wage war against this inner man. This language
will only fit the experience of a Christian. How could a
nonChristian have an "inner man" who longs for the things of

God? Paul teaches that we are spiritually dead as nonChristians. The inner man is the new spiritual presence of God in our lives.

Second, why would Paul say he delights in the Law of God as a nonChristian? Why would he, were he speaking as a nonChristian, say that "I am not practicing what I would like to do, but I am doing the very thing I hate" (verse 15)? Paul has already declared that with nonChristians, "There is none righteous, not even one . . . there is none who seeks for God" (Romans 3:10-11). The idea of a nonChristian who hates sin and longs to serve God is incompatible with Paul's theology of human nature. Even though nonChristians sometimes desire to serve God as they understand Him, this passage is clearly discussing the true God of the Bible and His Law.

The language of this passage simply will not fit with the idea that Paul is describing his struggle with law as a nonChristian. Neither is the context of Romans, which discusses spiritual growth both before this passage (chapter 6) and after this passage (chapter 8).

THE LAW AND CHRISTIANS

God usually waits for a period of time (varying in length for each of us) before He lets us come face-to-face with the law. We become conscious we are still in sin, even though we know Christ has changed us on some level. For instance, some of our attitudes may have changed early on with little struggle on our part. But in our actions and in other feelings and attitudes, change is only temporary or nonexistent. There is something sickening in our sin nature dragging us back to our addictions, our lusts, and our evil passions.

Some Christians report that they were delivered from addiction to drugs on the day they received Christ. This was not my experience. But I believe God can, and does, do such things. God has the power to miraculously deliver us from sin in a moment's time. When He elects to do so, we should receive such blessings with joy. But even if God does give a miraculous deliverance in an area or two, He will not deliver us from our entire sin nature that way. We may only be healed in one or two of the most destructive areas, while the bulk of our growth still lies ahead.

As we strive to obey God, we fail. We hope that we will not take the deadly turn toward legalistic dishonesty at this point. The most terrible and destructive reaction we can have in the face of moral failure is to claim we aren't really failing or to claim it isn't that bad. It is just as disastrous to claim it was someone else's fault. All of these reactions suggest the same thing: We are denying our deficiency before God's Law. We are guarding against admitting our inadequacy. Whether by rationalizing, minimizing, or blame shifting, we are refusing to learn the lesson God wants us to learn. These sin-denying tools are the stock-in-trade of the Pharisaic Christian. They only prolong and worsen a treatment that cannot be avoided.

We feel torn. On one level we want to obey God, and it gets pretty hard to understand why we still feel compelled to sin. This is how Paul put it in Romans 7:12-13—

> So then, the Law is holy, and the commandment is holy and righteous and good. Therefore did that which is good become a cause of death for me? May it never be! Rather it was sin, in order that it might be shown to be sin by effecting my death through that which is good, that through the commandment sin might become utterly sinful.

This passage is warning us not to blame our problems on the Law. The Law is without flaw, and it is operating perfectly. The problem is our sin nature and its rebellious reaction to the Law. The Law is merely bringing to light the reality and even the horror of that nature. This is what Paul means when he says that "sin might become utterly sinful."

As young believers, we think Christians are doing well when they *avoid* sin. After some years of this treatment, we

When sin has "become utterly sinful," we are in a position to admit our true helplessness.

learn Christians are doing well when they *admit* sin. Paul comes to this point explicitly in chapter 7 verses 18 and 19:

> For I know that nothing good dwells in me, that is, in my flesh; for the wishing is present in me, but the doing of the good is not. For the good that I wish, I do not do; but I practice the very evil that I do not wish.

What despair and pain there is in this cry! Have you ever felt this? I know I have. We might wonder whether Paul is losing his Christian walk. Is he on the verge of backsliding all the way to hell? Far from it! This is the cry of one who is learning exactly what God wants him to learn. This believer is coming to own the prerequisite to further depth with God. He is coming to the end of himself. He is realizing in a new way that he will never satisfy the righteous demands of God. He is also discovering that only helpless clinging to God in complete dependence holds any hope. Listen to the misery in Paul's words as he seems to reach a crisis of failure in verse 24: "Wretched man that I am! Who will set me free from the body of this death?"

Yet there is this sudden note of victory as well: "Thanks be to God through Jesus Christ our Lord!" (verse 25). Like life springing out of death, the author of this passage has found that dependence on Christ begins where dependence on self ends. The Law has done its job for the moment.

UNDERSTANDING THE PRINCIPLE

It's not enough to have felt the same sense of despair Paul does in this passage. We also must understand what it means. Why do we sometimes feel such despair, and why does God allow it?

Earlier we pointed out that both the Old and the New Testament contain imperatives, or instructions. There are things we should do, and things we should avoid doing. For instance, I should pray, read my Bible, and witness for Christ when I get the chance. But I should avoid needlessly hurting other people or becoming dependent on drugs.

As Christians, in our hearts, we want to comply with these instructions. However, our old natures, what Paul calls "the flesh," want to disobey these same instructions. This often creates an inner struggle that can be quite painful. In Galatians 5:17 Paul describes this struggle this way: "For the flesh sets its desire against the Spirit, and the Spirit against the flesh; for these are in opposition to one another, so that you may not do the things that you please."

As we focus on this struggle and intensify our efforts to see the Spirit triumph over the flesh, we grow more and more frustrated every time we fail. We may even resort to various forms of self-punishment and personal vows in order to gain victory.

Once we utter a vow, whether verbally or mentally, we are likely to fail again, because we have created a new law with even more authority and therefore more power to stimulate our flesh. We can work ourselves up into a frenzy of self-effort during these episodes, sometimes at the urging of our legalistic friends. But what is the result? We sin again. We fail. Even when we succeed, we lose the joy of what we are doing, because our motives center in the law. We are now "under law," and as God warned in Romans 6:14, sin will be master over us until we correct the problem.

Where do we turn? I am certainly not going to suggest that we shouldn't read our Bibles or witness, or that we might as well go ahead and get drunk. But if neither the law nor wanton sinning is the answer, where are we to turn? We are wretched creatures, aren't we?

People turn one of three ways in this situation, but only one leads to victory.

THE FIRST RESPONSE TO FAILURE: GIVING UP
Thousands are reached for Christ when they are students or young adults, but many lose their way and no longer walk with the Lord. Why does this happen so often? There is more than one reason, but I think one reason is more common than any other.

The most common reason young Christians lose their walk is that they fall into sin of some sort, and because they are also under law, they are not able to appropriate the grace of God. They become ashamed to face God and other Christians because they know they are guilty. They feel that what they have done is so bad that God and others would reject them if they were open about it. Terrifying sermons on the consequences of sin and books that threaten sinners with every sort of doom strengthen the impression that it is not safe to fail.

Christian leaders and older Christians must learn to recognize when young Christians are coming under this sort of performance bondage and be able to help deliver them from it.

While they may be right about other people rejecting them, they are wrong when they think God would do so. As we shall see, "There is therefore now no condemnation for those who are in Christ Jesus" (Romans 8:1). But the Accuser of the Brethren will urge upon sinful Christians the idea that God couldn't be too happy to see them after the way they've been living. Before long, all joy disappears from their walk with the Lord, and Christianity itself becomes too burdensome to bear. In sorrow, young believers wander away from Christian fellowship and try to drown out their disappointment in some distraction.

THE SECOND RESPONSE TO FAILURE: LEGALISTIC DISHONESTY

Some Christians turn a different direction when caught between the demands of God's law and personal failure. They begin to distort reality in such a way that they are able to avoid facing their problems.

Some develop a secret life that they live right alongside the public one. Publicly, they fearlessly denounce sin and wickedness. But privately, they may harbor bitterness or have some secret immoral sex from time to time. Pastors who work with outreach ministries have all met a fundamentalist with a dual life. It is very hard to understand why certain people (almost always from a legalistic religious background) are so fierce in their attacks on others for sin, sometimes fixating on even very minor infractions, only to turn up later involved in the most flagrant, but secret, personal sin themselves. The entire country has been treated to this spectacle during the past few years, as several famous, angry, sin-denouncing preachers have been discovered in gross perversion and even crime.

Hypocrisy is nothing new, and no one in Jesus' day was criticized more for it than the Pharisees. Ironically, no group in all of Israel was more radically committed to obeying the law than they. Observant Christians still notice the same thing over and over again today. It is not our mission to analyze fully why or how people are able to live such a contradiction. The secret dual life is probably a pattern learned in childhood and gradually expanded to include first one and then another area of sin.

> *By focusing attention on the horrors of certain sins, legalists hope to direct attention, including their own, to the sin of which they do not feel guilty.*

What happens when a legalist with a dual life rises at a Bible study to angrily deplore the wickedness of various areas of sin? Is it that these legalists are preaching to themselves, hoping if they are furious enough about sin they will finally listen to their own message? Is it that they "dissociate" (i.e., reality), entering a mental state that somehow fails to notice that they are just as guilty as everyone else? Or is it because, by issuing shrill denunciations on sins of which they are not exactly guilty, they hope to deflect attention from the area where they *are* guilty?

I believe it is usually the last reason.

This way, they don't have to look squarely at failure. Jesus said such people "strain out a gnat and swallow a camel" (Matthew 23:24). Often, the least important moral rules are continually stressed. These rules, usually the external ones, are not kept *along with* what Jesus called the weightier portions of the law. They are kept *instead of* the weightier portions.

Straining out the gnat and swallowing the camel is nothing but a tactic to divert attention from personal failure. It is one of the worst manifestations of hypocrisy and a sure sign we are focusing on law rather than grace. This practice is a product of training and modeling. Legalists do not exactly realize they are straining out the gnat. They are often the last to realize what they are doing.

Under a grace perspective, we can look directly into the heart of even the most demanding portions of God's law—like those that call on us to love God with *all* our heart, soul, mind, and strength; or those that call on us to love our neighbor as ourselves. We can safely look at the full demands of God's law only when we have given up trying to deny we fail to keep it.

Back when I was growing up, we had a lawn mower with no off switch. After using the mower, one usually laid the head of a hammer (wood-handled was the best) on the block of the engine so that it touched the tip of the spark plug. The result was instantaneous. The engine stopped as soon as the power to the spark plug was diverted in this way. Similarly, our spiritual growth may be progressing in a healthy way until the day we turn to legalistic dishonesty. That wrong turn will stifle true growth nearly as quickly as the hammer head stopped that old mower. We may see continued learning, minor outward change, and even victory in Christian ministry. But we are not growing closer to God until we have a change of perspective. We have developed a controversy with God that we need to resolve His way.

THE THIRD RESPONSE TO FAILURE:
WALKING ACCORDING TO THE SPIRIT

We have seen that, under the pressure of failure to keep the law, some give up while others take up the techniques of deception and hypocrisy, leading to Pharisaism. But there is a third path. This last reaction, the correct one, is "walking according to the Spirit," which will be the subject of our study of Romans 8.

LIFE UNDER LAW
OR UNDER GRACE

Before continuing our study of Romans, we should make sure we understand the difference between the perspective of one who is "under law" and one who is "under grace." If it seems we are pounding this issue hard, it is because abundant evidence suggests that contemporary Christians have great difficulty understanding the difference between these two perspectives. Legalism is a subjective state of mind, and therefore it is hard to describe in objective terms. It is easy to fail to recognize the earmarks of legalism in our own lives.

Remember, it's not that the law isn't there anymore, but that we are not *under* it. We might think of it this way: Being under law means I am somehow basing my identity on my performance.

Under law, I am drawing my view of what I am from what I do. Days of success make me feel proud and happy. Days of failure make me feel like Paul in Romans 7. But the main point is that I am not growing in grace as long as I live under this perspective. That's because when I am under the law, the basis for who I am is in me and what I can or can't do, not in Christ and what He has done. Interestingly, it is possible to think performance matters, even that it is important, without basing my identity on it.

DIFFERENCES BETWEEN THE LEGALISTIC AND GRACE PERSPECTIVES

Let's review the sometimes subtle differences between the "under law" perspective and the "under grace" perspective using a series of comparison charts.

> *Being under law means I am somehow basing my identity on my performance.*

TABLE 8.1

Area	Under Law	Under Grace
View of the law	A set of detailed obligations that I must keep Rigid application of case law	The underlying principles of the law describe the ultimate goal toward which God is moving me: a loving lifestyle.

As noted earlier, the believer under grace views the law differently than the one under law. Under grace we are interested in the ethical principles in the law—the big picture. Under law, the big picture is exactly what we don't want to see. It reminds us of our failure too much.

We have referred to straining out the gnat. Why was Jesus upset about this practice? Jesus didn't say it was wrong to tithe their mint, dill, and cumin, as the Pharisees did. But it is odd that they would think of doing it! How could people who are wrestling with the real moral issues of the law—like absolute devotion to God, love of others, and selfishness—find the time to worry about tithing their spice boxes?

The answer is that they did not do both. Rather than find time to cover the important things and *also* do the little things, they focused on the little things *instead of* the important things. Jesus said they "neglected the weightier provisions of the law: justice and mercy and faithfulness" (Matthew 23:23). The problem was that their focus was so centered on legalistic compliance with details of the law that they were missing the big picture. The underlying motive for straining out the gnat (whether conscious or not) is exactly that: to avoid looking at the big picture.

At a Bible study I used to teach I met a young man who had grown up in an extremist legalistic church. He was away from God when we found him, living in gross immorality, but he responded to God and returned like a prodigal son to his father. However, his legalistic attitudes were deeply ingrained. He found it hard to resist the urge to judge others for minor infractions of the law, and he would regularly point out people's sins to them and to others.

Ironically, at the same time he judged others for minor faults like saying an off-color word, he continued to struggle with sexual addictions he had developed during his excursion into the world. I began to notice how he would become agitated about someone in the group smoking or listening to rock music, only to admit days later (or have his partner admit) that he had again fallen into serious sexual sin. It eventually got to the point where whenever he started pointing the finger or giving little sermonettes about the evils of going to bars or cussing, I would look for a chance to ask, "Have you fallen into sexual sin again?" He almost always had.

Failure to value the things God says are important—and the corresponding tendency to harp on things given little emphasis in the Bible—is an almost certain sign of legalism. In legalistic systems, it is possible for members to feel they are doing well because they avoid certain areas of sin and have their daily quiet time. But the real truth may be that they aren't living for God at all. Legalistic systems usually play down sins of omission, like failure to love others, or invisible sins, like living for money. Yet there is a strange contradiction when it comes to certain chosen areas, where no slack is given whatever.

Perhaps this is what God faced when Adam and Eve appeared before Him in some sort of fig-leaf clothing. Before they could go far discussing their nakedness problem, God cut to the heart of the issue: "Have you eaten from the tree of which I commanded you not to eat?" (Genesis 3:11). It's odd that Adam and Eve would have concerned themselves with something like their nakedness when they had just failed the very essence of what God wanted them to do. God knew their fig leaves were pointless efforts to mask their sense of shame and guilt over their disobedience. Unfortunately, the human race has not left off sewing fig leaves, and now we often use the Law of God as our leaves.

TABLE 8.2

Area	Under Law	Under Grace
View of self	I am regenerate, and therefore I am able to keep the law. The law helps me live for God.	I am regenerate, but I still can't keep the law, because of my "outer man." By relying on the Spirit, not the letter, I can gradually change.

One of the easiest ways to discern whether people are under law is to find out whether they advocate focusing on the law because it is helpful for spiritual growth. Or do they argue that compliance with law is not the best way to grow spiritually? Some authors and teachers make it sound like we can simply face the law and do it now that we are converted. But Paul clearly draws a distinction between being under law and walking by the Spirit. For instance, Galatians 5:18 says, "If you are led by the Spirit, you are not under the Law." This is an either-or proposition. We cannot have both at once. Notice also that, in the context of this statement to the Galatians, both the alternative of being under law and that of following the Spirit apply to Christians, not to nonChristians.

The question is not whether God wants us to live a righteous life, but how He wants us to get there.

Of course, some Christian teachers do teach licentiousness. This would probably be very common in circles where the theology is more liberal. We are not arguing in favor of licentiousness. We are arguing in favor of grace, which is totally different. The Christian under grace looks to the power of the Holy Spirit, not the law, for help in living for God.

Licentiousness is not the cure for legalism any more than legalism is the cure for licentiousness. Both of these falsehoods are bad and cannot heal each other. Only a rejection of both and a decisive acceptance of God's position holds any hope.

TABLE 8.3

Area	Under Law	Under Grace
View of the Holy Spirit	Little practical understanding of the Spirit's ministries	Depends on the Holy Spirit for all power, motivation, and direction

No law-oriented Christian would say the Holy Spirit is unnecessary. But it is strange to see how rarely His ministry comes up in discussions about spiritual growth. Sometimes we get the feeling that the Spirit is being stuck on at the end, like tipping one's hat, rather than occupying the center of the discussion.

I remember studying systematic theology in seminary. We used a thick text that is considered mainstream evangelical theology. Our teacher pointed out with dismay how odd it was to find that this volume of over five hundred pages devoted less than two to the ministries of the Holy Spirit. The ministries of the Spirit seem to be receiving more attention today, but many have still not grasped that walking according to the Spirit and a focus on law are mutually exclusive.

TABLE 8.4

Area	Under Law	Under Grace
The "key" to spiritual growth	Self-discipline *or* Special experiences	Knows self-effort is futile (Romans 7:18) Looks to a process, not to quick-fix experiences

Sometimes people like to point out that one of the fruits of the Spirit is self-control (Galatians 5:23). They may overlook the fact that self-control is the *result* of walking by the Spirit, not the means to that end. In the minds of some teachers it seems like Galatians 5:16 must read, "Do not fulfill the desire of the flesh, and you will walk by the Spirit." In reality, the verse reads, "Walk by the Spirit, and you will not carry out the desire of the flesh." This distinction is not a minor one. It is the difference between cause and effect. It is the difference between law and grace. Is the power for change coming from me? Or is it coming from God?

The same goes for the many passages in the New Testament that extol various aspects of righteous living. These passages are all imperatives that depend on the indicatives; they call for our response to what God has done. For instance, James says, "Faith without works is dead" (James 2:26). Authentic faith will issue in good works because the Spirit will transform the one who walks in faith. But it would be foolish to think good works would issue in faith. We will see in the next chapter how walking by the Spirit issues in good works.

The tree of self-effort is a barren one indeed, especially to the honest Christian. Usually, Christians under law eventually sense this barrenness. In their thirst for relief from chronic failure, a vacuum is formed. Into this vacuum comes the promise of a special experience, an anointing, a healing, or the secret knowledge that will make everything all right. Just as some economically disadvantaged people are vulnerable to "get rich quick" schemes, the defeated, law-living Christian is highly vulnerable to shortcut plans that yield instant spiritual maturity or escape from personal problems.

Certain actions or disciplines are advanced today as the secret experience that can heal in a short time. Many of these experiences are perfectly legitimate in the right context. The problem comes when we view them as the cure-all or shortcut for fixing our fallen natures. Some may come to view a new form of worship experience as the cure-all. Others conclude that finally realizing how badly they have been victimized will set them free from their problems. Others determine they need to have some people lay their hands on them and cast out devils.

Unfortunately, none of these will provide a shortcut to anything, even though they could be helpful in some cases. We may experience some freedom from shame by exploring our victimization, but this is no missing key to instant growth. When, as defeated Christians living under law, we conclude this is the case, these experiences become a new legalism—yet another claim as to how we can keep the law. One who has demonic oppression needs deliverance. But this is no substitute for maturity. Moving worship of the Lord is a great experience. But it will not make us spiritually mature. It is only one aspect of the spiritually minded life.

> *There are no quick fixes for our fallen nature.*

We need to accept this once and for all: There are no shortcuts to spiritual maturity.

TABLE 8.5

Area	Under Law	Under Grace
Approach to Scripture	Relies on an inconsistent hermeneutic Unable to harmonize Jesus and the epistles	Is consistent and is able to harmonize the gospels and epistles

JESUS AND THE LAW

Modern legalistic interpreters often rely on Jesus' words in certain sections of the gospels to establish their law thesis. Jesus was indeed a teacher of the law. Galatians 4:4 confirms that Jesus was "born of a woman, born under the Law." He spoke in a milieu where people actually thought they were keeping the law. His first mission was to clarify the meaning of the law so people would understand how far short they were falling. Only then could His legalistic audience accept their need for grace. As modern interpreters try to make Jesus' statements about the law the centerpiece of New Testament teaching on this subject, they run into inconsistencies with reality as well as contradictions with the rest of the New Testament. These are often simply ignored or glossed over. But the correct interpretation is the one that explains all the material in the Bible, not just one passage at the expense of another. God has given us His Word, and the best way to avoid distorting it is to interpret the Bible in light of itself. God's program may change during different periods of history, but He will not contradict Himself.

Some law-oriented interpreters actually revel in the contradictions generated by their system of thought. One recent author comes right out and says, "The fact is, salvation is absolutely free, but salvation will cost you everything." This statement is not just a seeming paradox. It is outright nonsense. Suppose everything you have is one million value units. This statement says one million equals zero. If we feel no need to make sense in our interpretations, then interpretation itself is a complete waste of time. We might as well agree with the nonChristian world that "You can interpret it any way you want to." For that matter, we might as well forget about the Bible altogether, because we have no way of knowing what it means.

Let's take two examples of Jesus' teaching on the law and see how these should be harmonized with His own comments and the rest of the New Testament.

First, consider the Sermon on the Mount. Volumes have been written arguing that it is our duty to follow this sermon to the letter. Suppose we accept this argument. In the Sermon on the Mount Jesus says,

> "But I say to you, that everyone who looks on a woman
> to lust for her has committed adultery with her already
> in his heart. And if your right eye makes you stumble,
> tear it out, and throw it from you; for it is better for you
> that one of the parts of your body perish, than for your
> whole body to be thrown into hell." (Matthew 5:28-29)

This is fine ethical teaching. It is wrong to desire adultery, and such a sin would be bad enough to send us to hell. No wonder Jesus says we should pluck out our eyes if they are causing us to lust.

How many times, according to the New Testament, would we have to be guilty of lusting before we would be sent to hell? The answer is beyond dispute. Even one violation of the law guarantees that we fall short of the righteous standards of God (Galatians 3:10, James 2:10). Here the modern legalist says, "If we do lust, we need to be sure to ask for forgiveness." But that is not what Christ suggests, is it? He says we should pluck out our eyes! If we are under law for salvation, it's too late to ask for forgiveness once we have sinned. If we are able to be forgiven, we are under grace. But Jesus' sermon reflects law, not grace. He knew we first have to face the full demands of the law before we can appreciate grace. He was trying to convince His self-righteous audience that they needed the grace of God because they were sinners before the law. He summarizes the demands of the law in Matthew 5:48— "Therefore you are to be perfect, as your heavenly Father is perfect."

Yes, we do have to be perfect if we want to enter Heaven. But the key is to notice Christ's other promise: "Do not think that I came to abolish the Law or the Prophets; I did not come to abolish, but to fulfill" (Matthew 5:17). Jesus is our fulfillment of the law. This is the only conclusion that does not bring the law down to a level where we can keep it and still provides for the possibility that some will go to Heaven. We can either keep the whole law all the time, or we can accept Jesus' provision of grace. These are the two possible paths to eternal life.

By recognizing why Jesus spoke of the program of law, we discover that His program is identical to that of the rest of the New Testament. He sought to convince legalists of the hopelessness of justification by works. Even His own teachings, which often reflected pure grace apart from works, come into focus when we admit this distinction (see, for example, John 3:16, 4:10, 5:24, 6:29). Living in the midst of a legalistic milieu, Jesus had to spend considerable time redefining the law for those who mistakenly believed they were keeping it.

We can understand the strategy of Jesus' statements as well as those of the epistles only if we interpret them in light of the unfolding plan of total grace. Jesus came to bring freedom. His burden is easy, and His yoke is light. But to enter His freedom, the prideful ego of man must surrender, admitting helplessness before the awesome Law of God.

TABLE 8.6

Area	Under Law	Under Grace
Mental focus	My duty: to do what the rules require	Identification with Christ Personal relationship with God Loving others as a means of growth

Suppose I have my wife write down what she would like to see from me. Then anytime she wants me to do something I pull out that list. "Sorry, it's not on the list," I inform her, and head out to do something else. This would be an odd relationship, wouldn't it? Or let's suppose I begin posting rules in different rooms of the house. Whenever my wife is in the kitchen, she has to follow the kitchen rules; when she is in the bathroom, there are the bathroom rules; etc. Why does this type of relating seem so strange?

Surely it's because such a relationship would be rather impersonal. As persons in relationship, we usually have no need of lists of rules. We are able to respond to the wishes of the other (when we want to) based on our relational knowledge of what pleases the other. At those times when we don't want to respond, a list of rules won't help. If we interacted via lists of rules, our focus would be on the rules, not on each other.

Even in cases where a couple actually resorts to the use of rules while sorting out their relationhsip, this is never viewed as the final goal.

Having said this, we also need to speak against a mentality that views the Bible as a source book for things we don't have to do. The one who comes to the Bible with this agenda has missed the point badly. God gave us the Bible to help us serve Him, not to "get out of" doing His will. It is because we want to live for God that we need to come out from under the law. Our next chapter will begin to explore the right way to see God's will manifested in our lives.

God wants our focus to be on Him, not on a list of rules.

TABLE 8.7

Area	Under Law	Under Grace
Reaction to failure	Surprised and distressed	Not surprised
	Rationalizations, minimization, blame-shifting, and self-recrimination	Confident of God's acceptance
		Return to active dependence
	Vows to do better	

William Newall once said, "To be disappointed in yourself is to have trusted yourself." It is hard to find a flaw in that reasoning. The implication is clear. Those times when we are deeply disappointed in our performance are the times when we have lapsed into a performance mentality. Such disappointment leads to various dishonest and annoying tricks designed to help us live with ourselves.

How difficult it is for the law-living Christian to simply admit sin. To do so without qualification would threaten the person's identity in a way no one could live with. The only solution is to receive our identity from Christ and give up on the whole work-righteous identity-building project.

We have already mentioned the peril of new vows to do

better. These vows are routinely broken, and they produce even more alienation from God when they are.

TABLE 8.8

Area	Under Law	Under Grace
Reaction to success	Proud and intolerant of others	Humbly grateful Still able to empathize with those who fail Sees continued need for growth

Legalists often develop a disagreeable demeanor of self-righteousness. We are all familiar with this distasteful holier-than-thou attitude, and none of us can honestly claim we have never had it ourselves. It is easy to see why, as an essential part of our growth, God wants to wean us from a focus on the law. If we harbor delusions that we are able to do good in ourselves, we will never give the glory to Him, and all our friends will pay a nasty price for our pride. Not only this, but as long as we harbor these delusions, we will not be coming to the throne of grace with empty hands to receive God's healing.

TABLE 8.9

Area	Under Law	Under Grace
Reaction to success	External conformity, but increasing internal defeat and hypocrisy Growing cynicism and despair *or* Self-righteous externalistic comparisons—self-deception	Gradual transformation into a person with a measure of victory over sin and a spiritual mind-set A more loving person

The final outcome of legalistic thinking is either depression and defeat or aggressive Pharisaism, as we have already seen. The alternative is the faith-rest walk of the believer under grace. We now turn to Paul's description of this walk.

PART
TWO

GRACE
IN ACTION

THE THIRD REACTION TO THE LAW: DEPENDENCE

Until now, we have been studying the theory behind our new identity in Christ. Most of these truths have been somewhat abstract. In this section, we become quite practical. Just as Romans 8 is more practical than Romans 5–7, this section of our study will focus on applying these theories to daily life. We will examine daily living and our new identity in Christ. In particular, we will study in depth what it means to set our minds on the things of the Spirit rather than the things of the flesh.

THE FAITH-REST WALK
Christians confronted with failure before the Law of God react in one of three ways. We have already discussed the two negative options: despair, leading to apathy or even apostasy; or denial, leading to Pharisaism.

But what about the other option? How *should* we react? If we understand this part, the doors will open wide for the unbelievable joy of what some have called the faith-rest walk with Christ. This is the ultimate place of victory toward which God is slowly guiding us. We will see the power of the Holy Spirit working through us as we relate to God and others with real love. There will be a freedom from self-absorption we have never seen before. In its place will be the knowledge of our real significance and purpose: not just pie in the sky someday, but a truly attainable walk with God where we are able to confidently "rest" in the security of Christ's love.

The author of Hebrews says, "The one who has entered His rest has himself also rested from his works, as God did from His" (4:10). When we leave off trying to establish our identity through our own good works, we can finally relax, and through faith depend on God for our lives. This security will also free us to open ourselves to the unbelievable experience of allowing God's power to surge through us in blessing to others. This supernatural lifestyle is also called walking according to the Spirit.

WALKING ACCORDING TO THE SPIRIT: THE BASIS, THE MEANS, AND THE GOAL

Walking according to the Spirit is the subject of Romans 8. The Apostle Paul summarizes it in verses 1-4:

> There is therefore now no condemnation for those who are in Christ Jesus. For the law of the Spirit of life in Christ Jesus has set you free from the law of sin and of death. For what the Law could not do, weak as it was through the flesh, God did: sending His own Son in the likeness of sinful flesh and as an offering for sin, He condemned sin in the flesh, in order that the requirement of the Law might be fulfilled in us, who do not walk according to the flesh, but according to the Spirit.

OUR BASIS: SECURITY

We will sometimes fail, but God wants us to know that "there is . . . no condemnation for those who are in Christ Jesus." Suppose my beloved wife asked me to change in some way. Probably, since our relationship is a loving one, I would be inclined to try to accommodate the request as long as it wasn't inappropriate. But suppose, as she asks me, she lays a .45-caliber semiautomatic on the table. I think it would put a real chill on the conversation! I would want to stop talking about her request and say, "Wait a minute. What's that for?"

> *The first thing we have to know as we move forward to appropriate our new identity is that we are secure.*

This illustration highlights the importance of moving toward God in the unshakable knowledge of our unconditional acceptance in Him. God lays no .45 on the table when He asks us to respond to His love.[1] He wants us to come to Him and follow Him out of love, not fear. This is why the Apostle John says, "There is no fear in love; but perfect love casts out fear, because fear involves punishment, and the one who fears is not perfected in love" (1 John 4:18). God is not going to reject us. Unless we know this we will not be able to rest in faith.

Our Means: The Finished Work of Christ
The next step is to realize that God has already done it all. In Romans 8:2-3 Paul says, "For the law of the Spirit of life in Christ Jesus has set you free from the law of sin and of death. For what the Law could not do, weak as it was through the flesh, God did." This is a restatement of what we have called "the indicative." That is, God always starts with what He has already done and then moves to our response to that truth. This is the pattern of grace: "Because God has acted, I want to respond." The pattern for law is the opposite: "*If* I act, God will respond." Who is the doer, and who is the responder? This is the first and biggest question, and one which we have already dealt with adequately.

Our Goal: Christlike Character
But now we move to another question. What should be my response to security in Christ? To that question, Paul answers

that God did what He did "in order that the requirement of the
Law might be fulfilled in us, who do not walk according to the
flesh, but according to the Spirit." This verse promises that the
requirements of the law—goodness, or righteous deeds—will
be evident in the lives of those who learn to walk according to
the Spirit. As we saw earlier, walking Christians will end up
doing the very things the Law calls for, but we arrive there via
a different, or indirect, path. This distinction is an important
one. It is neither double-talk, nor a subtle reversal of what has
gone before, as we shall see.

WALKING ACCORDING TO THE SPIRIT OR FLESH: DEFINITION

In the following verses, Paul repeatedly defines for us what he
means by walking according to the Spirit.

> For those who are according to the flesh *set their minds*
> on the things of the flesh, but those who are according to
> the Spirit, [*set their minds on*] the things of the Spirit.
> For the *mind set on* the flesh is death, but the *mind set*
> *on* the Spirit is life and peace, because the *mind set on*
> the flesh is hostile toward God; for it does not subject
> itself to the law of God, for it is not even able to do so.
> (Romans 8:5-7, emphasis added)

Over and over again Paul stresses that walking according
to the flesh or the Spirit is a matter of our mind-set. Before any
struggle in our behavior, there is a struggle in our thought life.
The mind is the true battleground when it comes to spiritual
things. What does it mean, in practical terms, to set our mind
on the things of the flesh?

WHERE WE GO FROM HERE

In the next few chapters, we will look at several major areas of
mental focus, or mind-set, that would constitute "walking according to the flesh." Several surprises may confront us during this

study. We may find that setting our minds on the things of the flesh includes things we never considered a problem. There might even be some areas of fleshly focus that we have mistakenly defined as "good." We have already seen one example of this: focusing on the law. Though many Christians believe focusing on rules is God's will, we are surprised to learn in Romans that focusing on the law is looking back to what we were in Adam. Other areas that constitute a fleshly focus may be no less surprising.

When we turn to focusing on the things of the Spirit, we are faced by the familiar: the so-called means of growth, like prayer, Scripture, fellowship, self-giving love of others, and the discipline of the Holy Spirit. But we may find surprises here as well. It is not enough to focus on the things of the Spirit if we do so from our old identity in Adam.

Our study will go beyond defining the means of growth. We will ask, "What is the difference between approaching these means from a performance perspective and approaching them in our new identity?" We have argued all along that the key is to see our "doing" arising out of our "being." We will now see that this crucial distinction means the difference between boring and deadening repetition of religious disciplines and authentic spiritual power for change.

DEFINITIONS: WHAT IS FOCUSING ON THE FLESH?
As Paul describes his struggle with defeat before the Law of God in Romans 7:14-24, what is his mental focus? Three things stick out:

- ♦ "I" or "Me"
- ♦ "That which I am doing"
- ♦ That which the Law says

His orientation is on himself and his performance before the Law of God. Now let's compare these to his own list of things to which we died in Christ.

TABLE 9.1

Paul's Mental Focus in Chapter 7	Things to Which We Have Died
"I" or "Me"	We died to our old selves (6:6).
"That which I am doing"	We died to sin (6:11).
"That which the Law says."	We died to the Law (7:6)

Isn't it interesting that these two lists match each other exactly? We will suggest that: Walking according to the flesh means we set our minds on those things to which we died in Christ.

If this definition is accepted, it seems clear that the experience Paul is describing in Romans 7 would be considered walking according to the flesh.

> *Walking according to the flesh means we set our minds on those things to which we died in Christ.*

When God says we have died to our old self, to sin or to the law, and we nevertheless set our minds on these things, we are focusing on our old identity—our identity in Adam. We are setting our minds on the things of the flesh.

In addition to the three things detailed in Romans 7, we could add another thing to which Paul says we have died. In Galatians 6:14 Paul says, "But may it never be that I should boast, except in the cross of our Lord Jesus Christ, through which the world has been crucified to me, and I to the world." Setting our minds on the "world" (Greek, *kosmos*) is yet one more mind-set that constitutes walking according to the flesh. We will briefly consider each of these possible fleshly focuses topically, before considering the alternative mind-set—that which focuses on the things of the Spirit.

NOTE

1. We should be aware that the *King James Version* has a different reading for verse 1: "There is therefore now no condemnation to them which are in Christ Jesus, *who walk not after the flesh, but after the Spirit*" (emphasis mine). The

last phrase puts a condition on the promise, giving it a completely different meaning. If this reading were correct, our acceptance would depend on our ability to walk after the Spirit and, apparently, would be removed if we walked after the flesh. However, this reading is mistaken. The last phrase belongs in verse 4 and was incorrectly copied onto the end of verse 1. None of the earliest and best manuscripts have this reading. However, the most ancient manuscripts were not available at the time the *King James Version* was written. Remarkably, there are very few errors of this kind in the New Testament. Of course, those of us who believe that the Bible was inspired and without error when originally written know there are some copyist errors in every manuscript we have. This doesn't affect the reliability of the Bible, because by comparing the thousands of ancient manuscripts in our possession we can determine with a high degree of accuracy what the originals said. Besides, the errors in copying hardly ever affect the meaning of the text in any significant way. However, this particular error in the *King James Version* is one of the worst. It does distort the meaning of this important unconditional promise. The *New King James Version* has correctly noted that this reading is an error. The truth is, there is no condemnation for those who are in Christ Jesus.

CHAPTER 10

WALKING ACCORDING TO THE FLESH: SELF-FOCUS

What does it mean to set my mind on self? Obviously, we can't help thinking of ourselves. But are we focusing on our old selves or on ourselves as we are in Christ? What did the Apostle Paul mean when he said, "Not I, but Christ"? Perhaps the following comparisons will help. Although the frame of mind on the left in the chart may sound like the outlook of a nonChristian, we can also think this way as Christians. In fact, if we are honest, we will have to admit that we do think this way much of the time.

TABLE 10.1

Old Self (in Adam)	New Self (in Christ)
Alienated from God—Therefore, we think of our old self on a horizontal plane—me versus my problems, others, circumstances, etc.	*Alive to God* (Romans 6:11)—Therefore, we think of our new selves on both a horizontal and a vertical plane. Our interactions with others, our problems, circumstances, etc., are all considered in the light of how God is, or may be, working through them.

Old Self (in Adam)	New Self (in Christ)
Doomed to death—Therefore, everything is temporary, and temporary things are valuable. We spend our time trying to acquire or hold onto temporary things like material wealth.	*Guaranteed eternal life* (Romans 8:16-17,38-39)—Therefore, temporary things become only a means to an end. Only eternal things have ultimate value (like God, the truth, and people). Our stewardship of material and natural things in this life is important, mainly because these will affect our future lives with God.
Alone, with unmet needs—Therefore, we look to others to meet the hunger of loneliness by loving us the right way. Much of our thought lives are spent trying to understand why others won't meet our needs or how to make them meet our needs. In our pain, we pity ourselves and are often angry at God and others.	*In union with Christ and with other Christians, our needs met fully in Christ* (Romans 12:5, Ephesians 1:3)—Therefore, our focus is on how we can meet the needs of others. Instead of pitying ourselves, we find ourselves praising God for His provision.
Unclear sense of identity—Therefore, we doubt our own significance and spend time seeking acceptance and affirmation from other people who assure us we are important people. We spend much of our thought lives fretting about what others think of us.	*Identity based on God's view of us* (Romans 8:31)—Therefore, we become less concerned about what others think of us. We are able to leave the question of who we are behind, as a settled matter, and direct our thoughts outward, increasingly free from self-doubt and man pleasing.
Guilty of sin—We *feel* guilty because we *are* guilty. When our mind is set on the old self, we experience an abiding sense of shame that depresses and robs us of motivation. Our focus locks increasingly onto self, interfering with our relationships.	*Forgiven completely, dead to sin* (Romans 8:1)—We are able to look away from sin, laying it aside at the cross of Christ. Our thought life is spent contemplating how we may accomplish spiritual goals, not on earlier failures.

In biblical terms, people who are selfish, or self-centered, focus on themselves in their old identity in Adam. Or, to put it differently, those who are self-centered in the negative sense look to themselves in an effort to establish their own identity. They interact with others in a way that shows they want to use others to establish their own identity or importance.

To see ourselves only in Christ is, in a sense, a Christ-centered focus, even when we are thinking of ourselves. This is clear from passages like Colossians 3:1-3—

> If then you have been raised up with Christ, keep seeking the things above, where Christ is, seated at the right hand of God. Set your mind on the things above, not on the things that are on earth. For you have died and your life is hidden with Christ in God.

Here again, we see the command to "set our minds" on the things above, because that is where our new identity lies. This is a way to think of ourselves without being self-absorbed in the negative sense.

We saw earlier that the more we focus on our sin problems, the worse they become. Strangely, it's the same way when we focus on self. The more we focus on what we don't have and how we can meet our own needs, the more intense our dissatisfaction becomes. The more we focus on how to get others to meet our needs, the more unacceptable their attempts to do so become.

As our lives progress, we may become more and more demanding and more and more disappointed in people. Some of us will turn to anger while others turn to sorrow and withdrawal, but the cause is the same.

> *As we walk according to the flesh, we are looking to ourselves and others for something they can never do— only God can meet our personal needs for significance and love.*

Why not turn to God at this moment and offer to begin looking to yourself as being in Christ, and not in Adam? Of course, you will sometimes fail, but it is important to have the purpose in your heart to follow God in this area.

PROBLEMS WITH MODERN THEORIES

We have put self-focus in the category of walking according to the flesh. This position will cause consternation in some modern readers. Today in our culture, focusing on ourselves is viewed as the key to happiness and health. Today, people believe they will solve their problems by "centering" themselves or "gaining a sense of self."

According to these theories, my quest should be to find my true self and liberate that self from the layers of repression and abuse heaped on me by others. The key is to discover my inner child—the true me—and become my own parent. Only by attacking my shame-based upbringing will I finally throw off the negative labeling and repressive rules that hold me down (the repressive parent within) and find freedom to express my creativity and my "true" feelings. I need to champion the inner child so I can get in touch with feelings that have been shamed and denied to me for so long. Only then will I finally differentiate my ego from the undifferentiated ego-mass of my family of origin.

Although many professionals reject such theories, popular culture seems to be reaching a level of agreement rarely, if ever, seen before in this century. For example, author John Bradshaw,[1] who has been called the high priest of inner-child therapy, has written a number of books that have all spent time on the *New York Times* best-seller list, often as number one for months at a time. These are some of the most popular nonfiction books in recent history.

Christian thinkers are confused about these therapeutic suggestions. On one side is the observation that some people, especially victims of acute abuse as children, seem to forget sections of their early lives or idealize a past that is known to have been horrible. This is usually a sign of repression or denial—defense mechanisms that can threaten people's ability to stay in touch with reality and to relate to others honestly. Those who are reeling from painful childhood abuse may live in a numbed and unemotional state, or their lives may be filled with irrational, displaced rage or anxiety. Only the most extreme Christian leaders would deny that such denial states exist.

On the other hand, developments in this field have alarmed

most evangelical thinkers. Today, it seems, not only the severely abused but virtually everyone is considered a trauma victim on one level or another. What may have been needed to remedy some extreme cases of dissociation is now believed to be the key to everyone's life. Yet these recently discovered therapeutic or self-help procedures are sometimes suspicious.

Thoughtful evangelicals today worry that what began as a legitimate therapy for certain victims may be becoming a fad that puts self and negative past experiences at the center of personal growth. Christians have been quick to adapt the thinking of secular and New Age teachers, like Bradshaw, to the Christian therapeutic market. Re-parenting theories now turn out to be the crux of Jesus' teaching as well as the plumb line by which churches and teachers are judged. Yet several searching questions can be asked of self-restructuring and family-systems theorists:

◆ Are inner-child and parental-shame theories biblical? It would be wrong to claim the Bible has to mention something before it can be trusted. The Bible doesn't mention bulimia, but that doesn't mean there's no such thing. On the other hand, if freedom from parent-induced shame is the key to growth, not just for the severely abused but for virtually everyone, how did people get along for so many centuries without this knowledge? Bradshaw argues that Western culture just began to awaken from its patriarchal trance during the American and French revolutions, and that most of our important realizations have occurred since World War II! Is it possible that a discovery made in the 1960s and 1970s by largely secular and New Age thinkers is the key to personal growth for most or all people? If so, what good is the Bible—a "revelation" that completely missed this central truth?

◆ Many of the definitions given for "shaming" are so broad they seem to disallow virtually all parental discipline, even the categories of good and evil. Some authors, including evangelicals, have defined illegitimate "shaming" as "any statement that says there's something wrong with you." How can this definition from a recent evangelical book be reconciled with the fact that there *is* something wrong with us? How would Jesus fare in the face of such definitions? He said the world hated Him because He testified that their deeds were evil (John 7:7). His sermon decrying the Pharisees in Matthew 23 would apparently be shaming and labeling of the worst sort. He also warned that He did not come to call the righteous, but sinners (Matthew 9:13). Is there still a place for admitting sin without feeling we are either shaming ourselves or being shamed? If not, Christ has nothing to offer us.

◆ Is it appropriate to view ourselves as more or less ideal when we were preschool children? Isn't the notion that "I have to champion the true person I was as a child" based on the belief that people begin good and become bad because of repressive parenting? Bradshaw expressly affirms this as the basis for his theories. But how does this theory accord with passages like Proverbs 22:15—"Foolishness is bound up in the heart of a child; the rod of discipline will remove it far from him"? Such a statement sounds like the *antithesis* of modern inner-child theory. So, too, does the Apostle Paul's boast that "When I was a child, I used to speak as a child, think as a child, reason as a child; when I became a man, I did away with childish things" (1 Corinthians 13:11). The Bible teaches that children are born fallen and need to have their antisocial selfishness brought under control through training and loving discipline. Children view themselves as the center of the universe and think everyone should cater to their feelings. They can't tell the difference between their feelings and reality. Many Christian thinkers wonder whether modern theory is suggesting that this is the ideal we should all seek.

◆ Beneath the secular shame theories is the unproved assumption that all shame feelings originate from outside myself. Authors like Bradshaw decry the biblical notion of innate sinfulness as the worst sort of paternalistic negative conditioning. He is adamant that the shaming voices within are those of our persons of origin—our parents. But even if this is true *sometimes*, how do we know shame isn't also native to the fallen human condition? When Adam hid under a bush, he wasn't hiding from Eve, but from God. When we dare to assume powers that are not ours, including the right to be our own gods, we feel unavoidable hard feelings, especially when confronted with the true owner of those powers and titles—the God of the universe. This feeling, so universal and unavoidable, is shame. Why look only to our outer environment for the source of shame instead of realizing that much of our shame comes from the inner knowledge that we are sinners?

◆ According to inner-child theorists, the key to release from shame is entering into my own pain and rage. By finally feeling in a deep way my own feelings rather than those of my parents, I differentiate my ego from the ego-mass of my family. But this theory is not proven. Some people appear to dwell on their pain and rage in a way that is quite destructive. If we compared a list of biblical passages that teach the need to enter more deeply into our suffering and pain to a list of passages teaching the importance of gratitude, thankfulness, and worship, how would the lists compare? Isn't it true that, according to the Bible, the emphasis for most people should be on developing appreciation for what God has done, or will do, for us, not on dwelling on our misfortunes? At the risk of being diagnosed as "in denial," I would point out that even Bible verses on the role of pain and suffering focus more on how to endure and respond to pain than on any need to enter into it. Such an emphasis need not imply that Christians should practice denial. Paul, Christ, and others in Scripture acknowledged that they felt pain. We need to recognize the balance in Scripture, which is heavily weighted in the direction of our need to resist our native negativity, lack of gratitude, and self-centeredness.

Christians, like everyone else, have to think about themselves. But there is such a thing as self-absorption in the negative sense, and this is a form of setting our mind on the things of the flesh. Certain people may need to focus on themselves and their past episodes of abuse for a period of time. The rationale for this is that only when they reach a greater level of resolution will they be able to leave such things in the past for good. But for most people most of the time, God wants us to be liberated from a self-centered focus and develop a Christ-centered focus.

NOTE

1. I draw my descriptions of Bradshaw's material primarily from two of his books: *Creating Love: The Next Great Stage of Growth* (New York: Bantam Books, 1992); and *Healing the Shame That Binds You* (Deerfield Beach, CA: Health Communications, Inc., 1988).

WALKING ACCORDING TO THE FLESH: SIN FOCUS

We have seen that Christians have died to sin. Therefore, according to our reasoning so far, setting our minds on sin would be setting our minds on the things of the flesh. Yet some modern devotional teachers argue that the first thing we should do when getting together with the Lord is to think of every sin we committed since the last time we were with Him. They argue that after identifying our sins we can confess them and receive cleansing. This allows us to put our sin behind us.

The scriptural basis for this approach is thin, mainly relying on 1 John 1:9: "If we confess our sins, He is faithful and righteous to forgive us our sins and to cleanse us from all unrighteousness." This verse has gained so much importance in some popular Bible teaching that it is quoted in some churches every single week. It is odd that any verse would have so much importance, or that such an important truth would be taught in only one passage. And this raises doubts as to whether some modern teaching on this practice is biblically balanced.

In the first place, the Apostle John is not speaking to the issue of personal devotional time with God in this verse, but to a comparison between orthodox Christian theology and a heretical, dualistic ideology. By comparing the parallel construction of verses 6, 8, and 10 with verses 7 and 9, we see that the comparisons are between Christians and heretics, not between "walking" and carnal Christians. These heretics managed to deny all human sin by claiming that what we do with our physical bodies doesn't count because the body is not spiritual. John rightly denounces these heretics as liars and insists we must admit we are sinners before we can be forgiven.

The main point for us today is not that we must receive forgiveness for sins as we commit them but that we should seek to resolve sins that weigh heavily on our minds when we come to God. This is because, from *our* side, we are feeling shame over our wrongdoing. Confession means to agree with God. In other words, we admit that what we did was wrong and that it was our fault, not someone else's. We need to appropriate the grace of God anew in these areas. Psalms 32 and 51 along with parallel passages teach on the need to resolve unconfessed sin with God.

> *Technically, instead of asking God to forgive us, it would be more appropriate to thank Him for having already forgiven us.*

Technically, instead of asking God to forgive us, it would be more appropriate to thank Him for having already forgiven us. Otherwise, we may develop a sin focus in our prayer lives with God, or still worse, come to believe that the .45-caliber semiautomatic is lying on the table. This would have a real chilling effect on our relationship with God.

God is willing to take the risk of granting us full once-for-all forgiveness. For those interested, the chart on page 113 summarizes important passages on the subject. These verses, and many others, teach that our salvation is secure and our forgiveness is once-for-all at the time we receive the gift of salvation.

Will the knowledge that we are secure lead us to become soft on sin and take advantage of God's grace? If it does, we have not understood correctly. Even the Apostle Paul sometimes felt it was necessary to remind believers that people are going to hell because of sin, so it should never be viewed as unimportant.[1]

TABLE 11.1

Ephesians 2:8-9	Salvation is "by grace . . . through faith. It is not the result of works." If our forgiveness has to be gained by our confession and daily request, it is contingent on works we do. These verses will not allow that.
Ephesians 4:32	God in Christ "has forgiven" us. The tense of the verb here means forgiveness is a completed action.
Colossians 2:13	"When you were dead in your transgression . . . He made you alive together with Him, having forgiven us all our transgressions." If all our transgressions have been forgiven, why do we need to continue to ask for forgiveness now?
Romans 8:1	"There is no condemnation for those in Christ."
John 5:24	If anyone believes in Christ, he "does not come into judgment."
Hebrews 10:14	God "has perfected for all time those who are sanctified."
Ephesians 1:13-14	God has "sealed" us in Christ with the Holy Spirit. This was a wax seal placed on scrolls so they could not be opened before the time. It means we will not be lost before our entrance to Heaven.
Romans 8:29 and Ephesians 1:4-5	The term "predestined" means to set or fix someone's ultimate destiny. God has set the believers' ultimate destiny. We will be conformed to Christ, or made holy and blameless at Christ's return (see also Philippians 3:21).

Sin *is* important, so much so that Christ died to forgive it. But the sad irony is that if we develop a sin focus in our lives, we fall ever deeper into the grip of sin, like a man struggling in quicksand. This was Paul's fate in Romans 7:14-24 before he looked away from "that which I am doing" and onto Christ. The power to be set free from sin comes, not from dwelling on how bad it is, but by dwelling on the "things of the Spirit."

We can also focus on sin, not because we feel bad about our sin, but because we want to sin. We spend time lusting and thirsting for opportunities to commit various sins, or reminiscing about favorite sin episodes of the past. These periods also constitute a mind-set on the things of the flesh. It is probably not necessary to say a great deal about this since it is so obvious.

Clearly, the key to these situations is the ability to turn our attention to something more positive, something of the Spirit.

A CORRECTED FOCUS

We have already seen that God wants us to "present [ourselves] to God as those alive from the dead" (Romans 6:13). This means we come to Him not focusing on our sins but on who we now are in Christ. We saw that the key to walking according to the Spirit is to set our minds on the things of the Spirit. But sin is a thing of the flesh, not a thing of the Spirit. To set our minds on sin is to set our minds on the things of the flesh. We have already acknowledged that there are times when we are bothered by unresolved sin and need to confess it and thank God for our forgiveness. But this is different from having a sin focus.

> *Instead of sitting down with the Lord and counting up all our sins, we should try sitting down and counting up all the things He has done for us!*

Many of us would do well to change our approach to our devotional times. Instead of sitting down with the Lord and counting up all our sins, we should try sitting down and counting up all the things He has done for us!

We should review the miracle of forgiveness and our marvelous new identity. We should express thanks and praise for who we are in Christ. We may very well need to review, consciously and even verbally, the truths of our identification with Christ. It is a good idea to state to God, "I'm not coming to you based on any of my works, which I know are sinful, but entirely based on the grace of Christ."

This is Paul's point in Philippians 4:8, which *is* discussing our devotional prayer lives: "Finally, brethren, whatever is true, whatever is honorable, whatever is right, whatever is pure, whatever is lovely, whatever is of good repute, if there is any excellence and if anything worthy of praise, let your mind dwell on these things."

Some Christians are virtually obsessed with their sins, and

every time they look to God the only thing they can think of is all the sins they have committed. (Of course, others are so self-righteous they hardly notice their own sin, which is a different problem.) When we are obsessed with sin, we are seeing the sin focus at its worst, completely disrupting our relationship with our Lord and condemning us to a miserable life of walking according to the flesh. No wonder Satan, the accuser, is so intent on pressing our sins upon us, as though our identity had never changed. We will all face an ongoing struggle as we attempt to look away from what we have done and toward what God has done for us.

NOTE

1. First Corinthians 6:9-11, Ephesians 5:5-7, Galatians 5:19-21. In each of these passages, the reasoning is the same. Paul is not threatening the believer with hell. He is arguing that, since people are going to be judged and sent to hell for such actions, what place do such actions have in our lives? Yet, it is clear that in Corinth they were actually engaging in some, if not all, of the behaviors he mentions. Paul argues that, though believers might do such things, it is totally inappropriate because "you were washed, but you were sanctified, but you were justified in the name of the Lord Jesus Christ" (1 Corinthians 6:11). Likewise in Ephesians 5:5-8 he lists some sins and says, "Let no one deceive you with empty words, for because of these things the wrath of God comes upon the sons of disobedience." Is he threatening his readers? No! He goes on to say, "Therefore do not be partakers with *them*" (emphasis added). It must be possible to partake in these deeds or there would be no reason to write this passage. But even though it would be possible for a Christian to partake in the deeds of darkness, his identity would not become "a son of disobedience." On the contrary, Paul reminds them, "For you were formerly darkness, but now you are light in the Lord; walk as children of light" (verse 8). Our identity is forever set, and therefore, we should not want to behave like those who have the other identity. The thinking here is consistent throughout the New Testament.

CHAPTER 12

WALKING ACCORDING TO THE FLESH: *KOSMOS* FOCUS

We saw earlier that through the cross of Christ "the world has been crucified to me, and I to the world" (Galatians 6:14). If, according to Romans 8:4-8, setting our minds on the things of the flesh means setting our minds on things to which we have died in Christ, this would include the world system. The term *world* (*kosmos* in Greek) is a special word in the New Testament. In most uses, the *kosmos* refers not to the *world* in the sense of the physical globe, but to a system of values. In 1 John 2:15 God says,

> Do not love the [*kosmos*], nor the things in the [*kosmos*]. If anyone loves the [*kosmos*], the love of the Father is not in him. For all that is in the [*kosmos*], the lust of the flesh and the lust of the eyes and the boastful pride of life, is not from the Father, but is from the [*kosmos*].

Kosmos describes the perspective of humankind without God, as well as the system humans have developed apart from God's leadership. The world system values temporary things like money, prestige, and sensual experience more than it does eternal things. Therefore, it stands opposed to God's value system.

Strangely, even Christians' value systems are sometimes based on things like the boastful pride of life, the lust of the eyes, and the lust of the flesh. Modern Christians often have difficulty seeing what is wrong with valuing the *kosmos*, even though God reserves some of His strongest words to warn us not to love it, such as those in James 4:4—"Do you not know that friendship with the [*kosmos*] is hostility toward God?"

One reason for such strong language is the fact that the *kosmos* is really the Kingdom of God's enemy, Satan. Repeatedly in the New Testament, Satan is called the ruler of this *kosmos* (John 12:31, 14:30, 16:11). In Ephesians 6:12 demons who are the "world rulers" of this darkness are called the *kosmoskrators*. John says, "The whole [*kosmos*] lies in the power of the evil one" (1 John 5:19). No wonder God is not pleased when His followers adore the system ruled by His enemy, the destroyer of human souls!

Things like money, pleasure, and career have a certain value, and we are free to enjoy them in the right context. However, each can become an idol, replacing God in our lives with an addiction.

> *No wonder God is not pleased when His followers adore the system ruled by His enemy, the destroyer of human souls!*

Let's take money as an example. There is nothing wrong with money per se, and everyone must make and use money. Working to earn money is the will of God (Ephesians 4:28). But in the *kosmos*, people look to money as their source of happiness and identity. As a result, it takes on an importance that is out of all proportion to reality. Some people are prepared to devote their lives to the acquisition of money, even to the point of ruining their relationships, their families, and their own physical and emotional health. Money is the idol of choice in North America.

A BASEMENT FULL OF FORKS
Perhaps if we change the terminology a bit, it will be easier to understand God's point of view in this area. Instead of thinking

of dollars, suppose we think of forks. A fork is made of metal, and most forks cost a certain amount of money. You could say that a set of a dozen forks has a certain value, especially if they are nice forks. They have not only resale value but utilitarian value when we are eating food. Therefore, it is doubtful that any of us would argue that forks are without value. Neither would we say it is a sin to own forks. In fact, all of us probably have some forks in our homes.

But suppose a certain man became fascinated with forks and began to collect them. Every day his fork collection becomes larger and larger as he steadily acquires forks from every source. Eventually, his basement begins to fill up with forks, until he is undoubtedly the biggest fork owner in the world. He realizes he owns millions of forks, including some very costly ones from Europe. Some of his friends chide him sometimes, arguing that there are better things to do in life than buying and collecting forks. But he just smiles. He knows they only say that because they have so few forks themselves. They're obviously jealous!

One night he comes home very late, as usual. His kids complain, "Dad, where were you? We wanted to be with you."

As he drags a wooden box in the door, he answers, "I found some great forks! Check out this whole crate I got."

Although they may groan in disgust, he only replies, "You guys just don't know the value of a fork!"

We may find this story laughable, but only because forks are neither an agreed-upon legal tender nor a common thing to collect. But the things we do collect are no different. Whether clothes, cars, real estate, sports equipment, or dollars in the bank, these could all be converted into forks. Jesus taught about a man who had spent his life filling seven enlarged barns with grain— another thing most of us wouldn't want today. But in that day grain was even better than money. It might as well have been forks, though, because when the man died he lost all of it anyway (Luke 12:16-21).

The legalistic thinker might speak up at this point: "I think anyone with more than eight forks in their home is wasting the

Lord's money!" But this is not the point. Whether you have fewer or more forks than I doesn't matter. What matters is that we have a sense of proportion in our lives—something our fork collector obviously doesn't have. We can buy, own, and use forks without falling in love with them or allowing our fork mania to interfere with our relationships and our Christian ministry. To put it differently, we shouldn't try to draw our identity from our forks.

Those who draw their identity from their forks spend all their time thinking about forks. This is the real point as far as God is concerned. People easily develop an unhealthy obsession for the things of the world. Then it becomes impossible to set our mind on the things of the Spirit.

FREEDOM FROM THE *KOSMOS*

John gives us one key to freedom when interacting with the world system. After writing about not loving the things of the world, he goes on to say, "And the [*kosmos*] is passing away, and also its lusts; but the one who does the will of God abides forever" (1 John 2:17). Here is the key to an effective critique of the world's value system. Only what is permanent is truly valuable, and permanent things are spiritual things.

Think about it. When you get to Heaven, what will be there with you? For one, God will be there. Therefore, God is an eternal value. Also, other people will be there. That means human beings have eternal, or ultimate, value. There are other intangible values that are eternal as well, such as truth. People who understand eternal values live for things like God, other people, and truth. They will sacrifice money, prestige, and personal comfort for the sake of God, other people, and truth. And they would never sacrifice God, people, or truth for worldly values.

What if someone offered you a million dollars to kill yourself? Not very tempting. What if he raises the offer to a hundred million? Still not tempting? It's too obvious! What good is a bunch of money if I can't enjoy it after I earn it? Suppose he says he will pay you now, and you can wait five hours to kill yourself, or even five hundred hours? I know I still wouldn't be tempted. How could I enjoy the money when I remember where it's all headed? This is the way our lives are if we live for the things of the *kosmos*.

An eternal value system makes sense, especially for a Christian. But how is it that our minds continually slip back into the world's temporal value system?

Within each of us is a deep-seated desire to feel loved and significant. In our lostness we learn to divert this thirst to things like money, acclaim, prestige, and sensual experience. None of these can really meet our inner needs, but like heroin to the junkie, they ease the pain for a while. We live in an age often characterized by secular thinkers as an age of freedom. But the truth is, we live in an age of addiction. As people, including Christians, try to satisfy their inner needs through the value system of the *kosmos*, they become more and more thirsty and obsessed.

> *As people, including Christians, try to satisfy their inner needs through the value system of the* kosmos, *they become more and more thirsty and obsessed.*

Even focusing on outwardly spiritual things could be part of a *kosmos* focus, because our motives might be recognition, prestige, or even money. There is nothing unusual about preachers who appear to be acting from worldly motives. All of us have heard someone boast about spiritual accomplishments.

Though we may have become Christians, fixation on the things of the world will not easily disappear. Most of us spend a substantial part of every day mentally focused on the things of the *kosmos*. All of that time is time spent walking according to the flesh, because our minds are set on the things of the flesh.

ASSESSING HONESTLY

What's the solution? Withdrawal to a monastery where our thinking won't be invaded by the world's evil? No. This is human thinking again—seeking to control the inward attitude by controlling the outer environment. Paul deplores any attempt to escape evil via withdrawal from the *kosmos*. In 1 Corinthians 5:9-10 he says,

I wrote you in my letter not to associate with immoral people; I did not at all mean with the immoral people of this [*kosmos*], or with the covetous and swindlers, or with idolaters; for then you would have to go out of the [*kosmos*].

It was immoral *Christians* he wanted them to avoid, as a form of discipline. Clearly, it would be unthinkable to avoid immoral nonChristians, because this would mean going "out of the [*kosmos*]." We would be depriving the *kosmos* of the very light it needs. This is also why Jesus said, when praying for His disciples, "My prayer is not that you take them out of the [*kosmos*] but that you protect them from the evil one" (John 17:15, NIV).

> Trying to escape the kosmos *is not the answer.*

OVERSEEING OUR MIND-SET

Recognizing that we spend much of our time with our mind set on the things of the flesh can be depressing. But all is not lost. We need to avoid making matters worse by reacting improperly.

The key to progress is not to count up the minutes we spend focused on the things of the Spirit or the flesh. Instead, we should learn to look away from any such scorekeeping and simply focus on Christ. Otherwise we will come under a new legalism.

God gives us information about the importance of our mind-set so we will understand the direction we need to take, not so we will begin constantly taking our spiritual temperature. If we focus on our performance in this area, we become spiritual hypochondriacs. Hypochondriacs worry and fuss about their health instead of simply doing healthy things and letting God and nature do the rest.

The fact is, God never says we have to log more hours focusing on the things of the Spirit than on the things of the flesh in order to grow spiritually. The ratio between these two is never specified. When we realize we are focusing on the things of the flesh, we have the opportunity to immediately change our focus to the things of the Spirit. If we sit fretting about how little we have focused on God lately, or how long or how deep our latest excursion into the flesh has been, we prolong the time spent walking in the flesh. We should quit worrying and immediately reestablish fellowship with our waiting Father.

THE CUMULATIVE EFFECT

No matter how little time I spend truly focused on the things of the Spirit during a given day, that time counts! During that time I have released the power of the Spirit into my thinking and my life, and He will work accordingly. If I do the same the next day, He will work again. At the end of a year, these moments with God may add up to an embarrassingly small amount of time. Yet God has been free to work unfettered during this time, and the result will be tangible.

After another year the amount of time spent with God will be larger, and after five or ten years it may be substantial. I will find that God has worked during these times, often so slowly as to seem imperceptible. After ten years, the changes in my life will probably be quite perceptible, unless the whole process has consistently been short-circuited by some grace-slaying perspective I might harbor—especially legalism or rebellion.

Are we prepared to come before God at this moment and admit we have spent entirely too much time trying to deny our fleshliness or fretting over how helpless we feel? Are we prepared to set these thoughts aside and immediately reach out to accept the hand God is offering us? Can we depart from the negativity of legalistic apathy and again surrender to the love of God like we used to? If so, we are ready to consider what is involved in walking according to the Spirit.

WALKING ACCORDING TO THE SPIRIT: PRAYER

God has provided various channels, or means, through which we can mind the things of the Spirit. The Bible teaches that God's blessing will come into our lives, not mainly in some general mystical way through the spiritual ether, but through these channels or means of growth. We will be focusing on four: prayer, the Bible, Christian fellowship (including personal ministry), and the discipline of the Holy Spirit.

OUR APPROACH

We have argued up to this point that legalism is a deadly threat to authentic spiritual growth. This is never more true than when we set our minds on the things of the Spirit through the means of growth.

Under the legalistic paradigm, these means of growth become, not ways to receive the power of God, but duties that seem to pump power up from within ourselves or that rack up Brownie points. Often the picture is completed with a menacing collection of threats and dangers for those who fail to partake of these means of growth in sufficient measure. These threats create the fear needed for motivation in the legalistic thought system.

We need to rethink each of the means of growth, considering not only how they should be viewed, but also how they should *not* be understood. For every thesis there is an antithesis. And the antithesis of God's program of growth in love is the legalistic model of tooth-gritting adherence to a code while bobbing and weaving to avoid dangerous sanctions along the way. Put differently, God's program is doing arising out of being. Legalism is when we *do* in order to *be*. Let's see how these two antithetical approaches to growth look next to each other.

PRAYER: DIRECT RELATIONSHIP

The Apostle Paul teaches that the key to walking according to the Spirit is to set our minds on the things of the Spirit. The most obvious way to set our minds on the things of the Spirit is through prayer. Nothing is more personal or more important in our relationship with God than our prayer lives. Our times of prayer also have the potential to be the most refreshing and reassuring times in our lives. Unfortunately, prayer is often portrayed as a formalistic exercise more suited to a machine than to a personal relationship.

Prayer takes a number of forms, including not only conscious thanksgiving, requests, and praise, but also a prayerful *attitude* of dependence where we practice the presence of God. This could be called an attitude of prayer.

THE ATTITUDE OF PRAYER

To set our minds on the things of the Spirit, we can simply turn directly to God in our hearts. Like turning over a mental leaf, it is not hard to bring God into our thoughts by turning our mental "face" toward Him. It isn't so much what we say at such times, but that we intend to interact directly with Him. Author Ole Halesby cites Revelation 3:20—"I stand at the door and knock; if anyone hears My voice and opens the door, I will come in to him, and will dine with him, and he with Me"—as a good description of prayer. Prayer is letting Jesus enter our lives, our minds, our situations.

LEARNING THE VERTICAL PERSPECTIVE

Every day there are disappointments, hurt feelings, failures, victories, and pleasures in our lives. How do we view these daily events and the feelings they create?

So often we find ourselves disgusted about what someone has just done. "I can't believe she said that! She's a real . . . !" we tell ourselves. Our struggles with others are often played out on the horizontal plane. It's me versus my spouse, me versus my boss, me versus my kids. The events in my life seem to swirl around in a jumble of often disappointing hurts. What am I doing wrong?

> *We can call this perspective the vertical perspective, because it recognizes that what God is doing is the most important variable to grasp and will give light to everything else.*

This is the horizontal perspective. God wants us to learn to look at our lives vertically as well as horizontally. He wants us to open the door to our daily lives and let Him into our thinking.

When our friend makes a mean comment, we can either spend our time reflecting on how bad she is, or we can step back mentally from the conflict and ask, "God, what are You trying to do here?" When we do the latter, we are considering our daily lives from God's perspective. We are interpreting our experience theocentrically (with God at the center) instead of anthrocentrically (with man at the center). We can call this perspective the vertical perspective, because it recognizes that what God is doing is the most important variable to grasp and will give light to everything else.

This is what Proverbs 3:6 says: "In all your ways acknowledge Him, and He will make your paths straight." Acknowledging God in our daily interactions—the vertical perspective—is a large part of what it means to walk according to the Spirit.

Choosing to raise the question of God's involvement is an act of faith whereby we combine prayer with our knowledge of the Word of God. When we look to God after our friend has hurt us and ask God what He is doing in that situation, various possibilities may present themselves. "Are You trying to press me into a deeper understanding of grace? Is this a chance for me to see something in myself? Is this supposed to be an opportunity for me to do something for this other person?"

As we bring God into our calculations, a new perspective on our lives is often accompanied by a general calming of our anger, fear, or hurt. Our personal reactions are still as real as ever, but there is a sense of calm that comes from realizing we are not living our lives alone and desperate, on the horizontal plane. Often, God will open our eyes to see things from His perspective. Have you ever felt a smile spread across your face as you realized the obvious truth of God dawning on your darkened and angry heart? It's downright embarrassing sometimes to realize how far we have been from God's perspective in our daily problems.

God doesn't always explain all of our pain, at least not on this side of eternity. Some tragedy can seem pointless for a long time. But the one who is abiding in prayerful desire to learn what God is doing is minding the things of the Spirit, and this will result in blessing.

> *Thoughtful Christians who bring their daily lives before God for insight are on a direct path to understanding and maturity.*

Sometimes we will shudder in embarrassment when we realize we have been struggling for hours or even days on the horizontal axis without even considering what God is doing. But there is no point in entering into a session of self-flagellation. Just determine that you will immediately begin to again bring God back into your thought life. Thoughtful Christians who bring their daily lives before God for insight are on a direct path to understanding and maturity.

The Spirit will call for our active cooperation in every situation as He shows us what He has in mind. But only those who are prepared to heed spiritual things will ever understand His mind.

GETTING OUTSIDE OURSELVES

One of the biggest barriers to direct fellowship with God is our inability to get outside ourselves. I knew a person who couldn't stop talking about himself long enough to relate to other people. No matter how hard I tried, I always had the feeling he had not listened to a thing I said, because he just kept endlessly talking about himself. As you can imagine, this guy had a lot of problems in his relationships. He told me his counselors said he was relationally dysfunctional. How many times I have listened to him go on about all his strange and varied hobbies and preoccupations, mentally shaking my head in dismay, wondering how I could help him. I often tried to explain the problem to him, but he didn't get it.

This must be the way God feels when He listens to many of us pray. We can't get outside of ourselves and into Him. We are turning to Him, supposedly for a period of personal relating, but all we can think of or talk about is ourselves, our problems, our desires, our conflicts, our disappointments, and our failures. Of course, there is a place for talking about all these things. But when our prayer is an obsessive self-centered monologue, all personal relationship is absent.

Most people thought my self-absorbed friend was annoying. At least with God we don't have to worry about that. His patience is infinite. But there is a problem when we come to God self-absorbed: We are blocking normal relationship. We are filling both sides of the relationship with one person—me. No wonder we often come away from a time of prayer with the sense that we weren't able to draw close to God!

What can we do to come out of our preoccupation with ourselves?

Hebrews 4:16 says, "Let us therefore draw near with confidence to the throne of grace, that we may receive mercy and may find grace to help in time of need." What does it mean to draw near to God "with confidence"? It means that instead of cowering before God in regret about how little time we have spent with Him lately, we need to simply resolve, "I may not have been with You much lately, Lord, but I'm here now! I'm going to immediately turn to spend this time with You."

If our kids could see into our hearts, they would know there is no reason to avoid coming to us with their problems. But instead of coming and sitting next to Mom or Dad on the couch and discussing their problems openly, kids often seem to turn inward, worrying about how we as parents might react. Most of us parents are vexed when our children are distant just because they are having problems. Wouldn't it be great if they could just quit worrying about how they look and open up fully at all times?

This is what God would like from us. But to do this, we have to come to Him as who we are in Christ, not as who we were in Adam. Do we think we love our children more than God loves His? We don't. But like our own children, we may be tied up within ourselves, lacking the boldness to throw our hearts open before God.

SETTING OUR FOCUS ON GOD

If we are having trouble getting outside ourselves and into God, some simple things may help. Try starting your time of prayer by commenting on some things about God instead of things about yourself. Just as you would not usually approach one of your friends spouting out about yourself, try holding back things about yourself with God at first. You know you want to talk about your own issues, but take a minute to get into God's issues. Who is God? What is He like? What has He done for you already? These are the questions we need to consciously and even verbally reflect on before Him.

Suppose you opened your eyes and found you were in Heaven, seated at God's right hand. What would your reaction be? You might well look around and say, "Cool! Thanks, God! I can't believe You've actually brought me here!" But Scripture says we *are* seated in the heavenlies with Christ. Why is there often little thankfulness in our prayers?

As we orient ourselves to our position with God, spontaneous praise is sure to follow. As we come out of our self-preoccupation we will realize who we are dealing with, and our entire demeanor and outlook will likely change. This is why there are so many admonitions in Scripture to constantly express thanksgiving and praise to God. These are not done for His sake. They do not meet any needs in God, even though He is pleased when we recognize Him for who He is. He must feel pleasure, if only because we have come out of our self-centered monologue long enough to truly relate to Him. Thanksgiving and worship are vehicles that help us get out of ourselves and into God.

After we have consciously centered our focus on the God who truly exists, we are free to speak of other things, like our own and others' needs. But isn't it interesting how some of our so-called needs are hard to remember after we have looked into the face of God? Often, other things will suddenly seem more important than our preoccupations.

We need to learn how to lay our failures aside and look away to Christ. He is waiting to enjoy personal time with us in prayer.

LEGALISTIC AND FORMALISTIC VERSIONS OF PRAYER

What does prayer look like under the legalistic mentality? One of the clearest warning signs is the presence of the twin brother to legalism—formalism. Formalism focuses on outward religious rites more than on inward heart attitude. Just as legalism seeks to reform the inward by focusing on outward behavior, formalism ignores the inward in order to focus on outward forms, like rituals and the observance of sacred calendars and liturgies. Of course, every Christian group and individual has forms through which, or within which, they express their faith. And any of these forms has the potential to replace a real heart encounter with God.

It is a well-known fact that many religions, including some that would call themselves Christian, are deeply involved in formalistic prayer. Instead of a time of personal relating with God, prayer becomes a ritual, a form to be followed. Just as you have to push a succession of buttons to get your money from an automatic teller machine, you have to follow various sequences of prayer disciplines to get your blessing from God. This is true whether these stages of prayer reflect where you are in your heart or not.

Sometimes people don't even bother to speak their own words, but instead let religious leaders write their prayers for them. This must have been the case when God uttered one of his clearest rejections of formalism in Isaiah 29:13-14—

> "Because this people draw near with their words
> And honor Me with their lip service,
> But they remove their hearts far from Me,
> And their reverence for Me consists of tradition learned
>   by rote. . . .
> And the wisdom of their wise men shall perish."

People are the same today. The religious mind likes to recite outward forms and formulas "learned by rote." That way, we don't need to put out the effort involved in relating personally.

When people become formalistic, they conclude that a certain sequence of words is what matters rather than the intent of their heart. It may be that people sometimes focus intently on the meaning of a memorized prayer or one that is written in advance. But it seems odd that we don't normally relate to other persons this way. The danger of formalism is high when we are not spontaneously and naturally communicating to God, but rely instead on prewritten or memorized prayers. In some religious groups, prayers are bought with money. Religious functionaries can be hired to repeat a prayer on someone else's behalf for a certain fee, even if that other person is already dead! This is odd when we consider that Jesus taught against meaningless repetition in prayer (Matthew 6:7-8).

In some Buddhist sects, the worshipers can spin prayer wheels as they enter a shrine. As the wheel spins, a printed prayer passes by a stylus, thus repeating the prayer over and over. A portable version can be held in the hand and spun like a toy. In this extreme type of formalism we see clearly the machinelike image of prayer, and by implication, of God. People wonder why God provided highly formalized worship in the Old Testament, if formalism is bad. The main answer is that the forms in the Old Testament prefigure Christ symbolically. Also, Old Testament believers had a different relationship with the Holy Spirit. One thing is clear: In the New Testament, forms and rituals are dramatically reduced. Further, believers are warned against returning to the Old Testament forms (Colossians 2:16-23, Hebrews 8–10).

DISCERNING FORMALISM

Such examples are rather extreme, but sometimes it helps to look at some of the more extreme examples in order to get the idea. We would be mistaken, however, if we thought formalism only appears in these more outlandish examples. In fact, it is very easy for any of us to lapse into formalistic prayer if we fail to consciously resist it. Sometimes the line between formalism and reality in spiritual things is harder to detect, and seeing it requires keen spiritual sensitivity.

Let's take a couple of examples. Many Christians find it helpful to have a short time of prayer before meals. First thing in the morning is another popular time for prayer, as is "when I lay me down to sleep." These regular parts of our day can serve as reminders to pray, and we are creatures of habit. Could these times also become formalistic? How would we know if they were?

Clearly, the mere fact that we pray at regular times does not mean we are formalists. Such a verdict would be a focus on the external in itself. But formalism is not a matter of the outward. It is a deeply inward state of mind—an attitude. To determine whether such practices are formalistic, we need to look deeper.

What is it about formalism that makes it objectionable? Simply put, formalism is impersonal. Formalists can go through their motions without ever addressing God personally. Therefore, we could pray at regular times without being formalistic, but if we find we are not making personal contact inwardly with God, then we probably are practicing formalism.

Imagine someone entering your living room and reading out a prewritten statement before turning and leaving. Is this a personal interaction? Suppose your neighbor stops by your house before eating each meal, sticks his head in your door, and rattles off the same few words before closing the door and leaving. Would this be personal communication? It might be, if you had dropped off his meal for him and he was just dropping by to thank you for it. But clearly it might not be personal. Formalism is truly an inward attitude, not an outward action.

Sometimes we mouth words of prayer at appropriate times without any thought whatsoever. When we are formalistic, we, like any legalist, can tell ourselves we have prayed several times that day, so all is well. Whether there is any personal reality to our prayer lives is another question.

ESCAPING FORMALISM

Escaping formalistic thinking is not always an easy matter. Changing the forms we operate under can give us an opportunity to reevaluate our outlook, but it won't solve the problem. Any form can become formalistic. We may pray very contemporary prayers at odd times and in strange ways but still be as formalistic as ever. This is because what matters is not the forms but how we view those forms.

The main thing to do when we realize we are relating to God formalistically is to repent and set out to reestablish personal rapport with Him at that moment. Again, each nonformalistic, real moment of fellowship with God counts, and such times will add up over the course of months and years.

I find that corporate prayer helps me avoid formalism. By joining into the thoughts of others, and by sharing my prayers with others, I seem to be able to focus my attention for longer periods of time. The perspectives of others challenge my own thoughts, causing me to come out of preconceived or ill-conceived notions and reconsider what God would want. Perhaps this is one of the reasons God calls special attention to the importance of corporate prayer (Matthew 18:19).

WHY PERSISTENT PRAYER?

The New Testament teaches persistent prayer. This means we should continue to pray over a period of time until God answers. For some, this is a stumbling block because it could be seen as favoring formalism. I used to wonder about this doctrine as a young Christian. Can't God hear a request the first time? Wouldn't it demonstrate more faith if we just asked once, trusting that He had heard, and never mentioned it again? The answer is no. God says it demonstrates more faith if we come back to Him regularly with our requests. By insisting that we pray persistently, God teaches us to spend more time with Him.

Jesus was teaching on the need for persistent prayer in Luke 18. Luke records, "He was telling them a parable to show that at all times they ought to pray and not to lose heart" (verse 1). Then He told the following confusing parable:

> "There was in a certain city a judge who did not fear
> God, and did not respect man. And there was a widow
> in that city, and she kept coming to him, saying, 'Give
> me legal protection from my opponent.' And for a while
> he was unwilling; but afterward he said to himself,
> 'Even though I do not fear God nor respect man, yet
> because this widow bothers me, I will give her legal
> protection, lest by continually coming she wear me
> out.'" And the Lord said, "Hear what the unrighteous
> judge said; now shall not God bring about justice for His
> elect, who cry to Him day and night, and will He delay
> long over them?" (verses 2-7)

This parable seems like an outrage to many modern readers. How could Jesus compare this episode to prayer? The judge's motive was avoiding harassment, not love! How should we interpret this parable? Should we pray until we annoy God so much that He grants our request?

This parable (like some others) uses a form of argument popular at the time but rarely used today. It is called an *a fortiori* argument, which is different from arguments by analogy that we usually use today. In an analogy, two things are compared for similarity. The parts of the comparison need to match fairly well for the analogy to be convincing. In an *a fortiori* argument, one part of the comparison is similar, and one part is different. The similar part should match well, but the different part has to be as different as possible to make the argument convincing. The form of the argument is, "If this, how much more that?"

Let's look at the parable of the unrighteous judge in a diagram.

TABLE 13.1

The woman's persistent request	Our persistence in prayer	*Similar*
The judge's motives for answering	God's motives for answering	*Different*

Jesus even calls the judge "unrighteous," so He clearly is not saying the judge and God are alike. On the contrary, the fact that they are so different makes us realize that if this no-good judge would answer the widow, our loving Father would much more readily answer us.

But what is God's motive for calling us to persist in prayer? He is omniscient, so He already knows what we will ask. He is omnipotent, so He is able to answer the first time we ask. Yet, He wants us to persist. Why?

Persistence is not for God's sake, but for ours. One reason God demands it is our reluctance to pray. He knows we would not spend the time we need with Him if He didn't induce us to. Persistence benefits us for several reasons, but the most important is that the needs in our lives motivate us to spend more time with God in prayer.

IS IT MY DUTY TO EAT DINNER?
We need to view prayer as more than a duty or a chance to ask for things we need. Prayer is also one main way we set our minds on the things of the Spirit. Praying can therefore be synonymous with walking according to the Spirit, if only we approach it the right way.

Eating food is not something we normally view as a duty. It tastes good, it feels good, and it is essential for healthy living. Why view it as a duty when it is one of the pleasures of life? It's the same with prayer. If prayer is so burdensome that we view it as a duty, it often means we are coming to God under law, or in Adam. Our depression associated with prayer results from our faulty orientation in spiritual matters. When we understand prayer as it should be understood, we won't need dutiful threats before we can pray.

Of course, there are certain times when prayer may lose its joy for legitimate reasons. We may be depressed because of circumstances in our lives, and this is not necessarily a sin. We may be so busy or preoccupied that it takes a real conscious act of the will, even a struggle, before we can enter into meaningful prayer. When this is the case, we can go ahead and do the right thing, depending on God's power. If our motives are faulty, we can ask Him to straighten that out later, as we shall see.

CONCLUSION
Our discussion of prayer is not over. A full understanding of prayer is not possible without considering how it interacts with the other aspects of our spiritual lives. The following chart considers some of the interaction between prayer and the other means of growth.

TABLE 13.2 THE INTERACTION OF PRAYER AND OTHER MEANS OF GROWTH

Fellowship	Jesus gave corporate prayer a special place when He said, "If two of you agree on earth about anything that they may ask, it shall be done for them by My Father who is in heaven" (Matthew 18:19). Based on this promise, we may fairly conclude that Jesus is implying that corporate prayer is more powerful than individual prayer, if only because when two or more agree, they have a better chance of truly discerning the will of God. The prayer ministry of the church is one of its most important.
Ministry	A ministry weak in prayer will tend to be overly strong on human effort. What we cannot accomplish via the power of God, we will try to supply through our own power. As we lose faith in the effectiveness of prayer, we will succumb to the temptation to use force and compulsion on people in an effort to bend them to our will.
Scripture	We need to pray that God will take scriptural truth and apply it to our lives in a living way. If we have learned the Scriptures in good measure, God will find it easier to bring us understanding about what He is doing in our daily lives.
Discipline of the Holy Spirit	Cultivating the vertical perspective through abiding in Christ is a prerequisite for making the Lord's discipline effective in our lives. As we shall see later, those who will not take their trials to God in prayer—not just asking that the trial go away, but that they understand what He is teaching—will not benefit from the suffering they undergo.

CHAPTER 14

WALKING ACCORDING TO THE SPIRIT: SCRIPTURE

How do we "set our minds on the things of the Spirit"? One important way is through the Bible. The human race has been uniquely blessed by God. For us Christ was incarnated and died. But this is not all. God has also given us something more precious than money or fame: His Word.

Imagine an alien spaceship landing somewhere in a city. Thousands of people gather around the ship just like in the old sci-fi movies. Finally the aliens emerge—strange creatures, very advanced. "We have come to answer your questions," they announce. They hand us a book and say, "This is a book explaining our world and much of what we know about history, science, and so forth." Then they take off, leaving the book behind. Wouldn't that be an interesting book? People would line up for a chance to read and understand such a book.

But what we have is much better than any book imaginary aliens could possibly leave us. We have thoughts from the Creator of the universe. We have the history of His dealings with the human race. We have the Bible.

Considering how important the Bible is, it is surprising that many believers have learned so little about it. Some of us may think we need heart knowledge, not book knowledge. We may allow that studying the Bible is good, especially for those gifted in that area, but we may feel we are "not that way."

Perhaps it would help if we better understood the importance of the Bible from God's point of view.

SPIRITUAL GROWTH WITHOUT THE BIBLE?

The Apostle Peter exhorts his readers: "Like newborn babes, long for the pure milk of the word, that by it you may grow in respect to salvation" (1 Peter 2:2). Neglecting to learn the Word of God will always eventually result in a complete stunting of spiritual growth, according to the Apostle Paul. In 1 Corinthians 3:1-2, he recalled that he could not speak to the Corinthians "as to spiritual men, but as to men of flesh, as to babes in Christ." Therefore, he gave them the food of babies. "I gave you milk to drink, not solid food; for you were not yet able to receive it. Indeed, even now you are not yet able." The last phrase stands as a warning. It is sadly possible to be years old as a Christian but still be a baby spiritually. One way to know we are spiritual babies is when we cannot digest the meat of the Word. We are still living on milk.

In Hebrews 5:12–6:1 God says,

> For though by this time you ought to be teachers, you have need again for someone to teach you the elementary principles of the oracles of God, and you have come to need milk and not solid food. For everyone who partakes only of milk is not accustomed to the word of righteousness, for he is a babe. But solid food is for the mature, who because of practice have their senses trained to discern good and evil. Therefore leaving the elementary teaching about the Christ, let us press on to maturity.

Here it says, "Everyone who partakes only of milk is not accustomed to the word of righteousness." In other words, they don't know their Bibles. If we think we will mature without learning the Bible, we have a surprise coming. According to these passages, there is no such thing as a mature Christian who is "not accustomed to the word of righteousness." No amount of prayer, fellowship, or spiritual experience can make up for a deficiency in the Word.

THE USE OF SCRIPTURE IN MINISTRY

Today, Christian ministry seeks to foster evangelism and spiritual growth in Christians, but our approach often exemplifies Madison Avenue more than the New Testament. As a result, our evangelism is ineffective or seems to fade away, or we are reduced to holding a sideshow to attract the attention of unmotivated believers. Pastors and lay ministers are often left wondering how much real maturity their people have.

One difference between some of our ministries and those of the early Church is that they relied more heavily on the power of Scripture. Paul called on the members (not just the leaders) of the church in Colossae to learn their Bibles. He tells them, "Let the word of Christ richly dwell within you" (Colossians 3:16). This would not describe the level of Bible knowledge in some modern churches.

In 2 Timothy 3:16-17 Paul told Timothy, "All Scripture is inspired by God and profitable for teaching, for reproof, for correction, for training in righteousness; that the man of God may be adequate, equipped for every good work." Although many modern Christians feel they have found a better way, God still thinks His Word is the tool of choice for Christian ministry. Paul went on to adjure Timothy:

> Preach the word . . . with great patience and instruction. . . . For the time will come when they will not endure sound doctrine; but wanting to have their ears tickled, they will accumulate for themselves teachers in accordance to their own desires; and will turn away their ears from the truth, and will turn aside to myths. (2 Timothy 4:2-4)

Today, as then, Christians would often rather hear sensational stories about miracles or witches. But those of us with a burden for building others up in Christ should, like Timothy, focus on sharing the Word of God.

SPIRITUAL WARFARE AND THE BIBLE

Another area for which the Bible is essential in our spiritual growth is spiritual warfare. To oppose the Evil One we need every spiritual weapon God has provided. When Paul described the weapons of spiritual warfare, he referred to the Word of God in one form or another more than any other thing.

Can you pick out three separate items of armor in this passage that are the Word of God?

> Take up the full armor of God, that you may be able to resist in the evil day, and having done everything, to stand firm. Stand firm therefore, having girded your loins with truth, and having put on the breastplate of righteousness, and having shod your feet with the preparation of the gospel of peace; in addition to all, taking up the shield of faith with which you will be able to extinguish all the flaming missiles of the evil one. And take the helmet of salvation, and the sword of the Spirit, which is the word of God. (Ephesians 6:13-17)

The loin girdle of "truth"; the shoes, which are the "preparation of the gospel of peace"; and of course, the sword of the Spirit, "which is the word of God," all refer to the Bible. No other thing is mentioned so often in this list.

If we plan to step up and oppose Satan, we had better be able to handle the Word of God, as Jesus did when He fought the Devil (Luke 4:1-13). Every time Satan challenged Jesus to sin, Jesus replied with the formula, "It is written. . . ." Are we able to fight the Devil this way? Some of us are vulnerable because we don't know the Bible well enough to meet his attacks effectively.

THE BIBLE UNDER THE LEGALISTIC PARADIGM

I once went to speak at a retreat for a small fundamentalist church with a friend of mine who had grown up in that church but had long since moved to another city. Friday evening I gave an impassioned plea for spiritual growth from Romans 6. Afterward, I opened the floor for discussion, anticipating some challenging interaction from the small group of two dozen college- and career-aged believers. The first guy who raised his hand asked, "Uh, yeah, what's your view on predestination?"

I recoiled in shock. I hadn't spoken a word on the subject of election or anything related to it. This guy seemed to have not been listening! Politely, I briefly sketched out my position and looked to the others for discussion on growing in Christ. Another guy raised his hand. "Do you believe in eternal security?"

Again, I strained to keep my eyes from bulging too much in surprise. Why were they asking me questions that were off the subject? Had my lecture been that uninteresting? The rest of the discussion continued to turn on similar controversial questions, never returning to the notion of growth. Later, as we drove home, I commented to my friend about the odd lines of questioning we got. He chuckled and said he remembered that when growing up those subjects had come up in that group almost every week.

What was this? I have been in numerous situations before and since where the same thing happened. Instead of talking about something that mattered, we always seemed to end up discussing whether hell is conscious or whether there are more than three levels in Heaven. Predestination and eternal security are favorites.

This is what we might call doctrinal wrangling. It is similar to "straining out the gnat and swallowing the camel." Straining out the gnat is when people focus on minor moral imperatives in order to divert attention from moral failure in important areas. The practice of doctrinal wrangling accomplishes the same thing in the area of truth. Both groups and individuals practice it. Rather than face the stark reality of God's truth, doctrinal wranglers have a sporting debate while never seriously considering change in their lives based on the claims of the Word of God.

Of course, Heaven and predestination can be important topics in the right context. But when they are foils, designed to turn aside the sword of God's Word, such discussions take on an ugly, almost obscene appearance.

Why divert attention from what God is trying to say? Usually, the reason is legalism. Only a legalist feels the need to keep the discussion on "safe" topics, because only the legalist is in danger of accusation from the Bible. Showing believers under grace that they are wrong is not a problem because they can admit wrong without feeling their identities are being threatened.

JESUS AND DOCTRINAL WRANGLING

During Jesus' ministry law-living people tried to engage Him in meaningless prattle about what is permitted under law and what is not. We hear His exasperation when He addresses the multitudes in Matthew 23:16-17—

> "Woe to you, blind guides, who say, 'Whoever swears by the temple, that is nothing; but whoever swears by the gold of the temple, he is obligated.' You fools and blind men; which is more important, the gold, or the temple that sanctified the gold?"

Someone at the retreat I mentioned earlier might have asked, "Well, which is it?" The answer should be obvious. This whole line of thought is so stupid it's amazing anyone would have wasted even a minute on it! "You fools and blind men," Jesus cries. How could they be taking the spiritual discussion in Israel in this direction when there were real issues that needed to be addressed?

Legalism will invariably have a deadening effect on our knowledge of the Bible. We end up with a sort of knowledge, but it cannot give life. Some of us raised in evangelical churches know who Zerubbabel was, but we can't tell a balanced position from an imbalanced one. Some of us know James 2:14 by heart, but we couldn't bring out our Bibles and use them in real evangelistic or counseling situations if our lives depended on it.

A RELIGIOUS TEXT OR A PERSONAL LETTER?

Formalism is another manifestation of legalism in the use of Scripture. Anytime we read or recite the Bible for a feeling of blessing without taking the time to understand what it means, we are practicing formalism, which is a sign of legalism.

Other religions treat their religious texts formalistically. Most religions view their scriptures in a way that suggests that the words themselves are sacred. These are read and chanted, often with no attempt to reconcile apparent differences in meaning or to apply the content to daily life. The texts are often not touched by human hands, and a reading stylus is used to point to the words and turn the pages. The sacred texts of other religions are often not updated in translation, even though the public no longer understands the language from earlier times. It is the words, not their meaning, that is important. The fact that people don't understand the text is considered unimportant for some reason. It almost seems like these sacred texts are viewed as books of magic words or incantations that can be repeated in a mindless chant.

These tendencies have also been noticeable in the history of Christianity. Formalism has had a rich history in Christianity, with the older traditions leading the way. For centuries, the Bible was unavailable to the public because the Latin Vulgate version was considered the only one sanctioned by God. One wonders why God was able to learn Latin but not German or French!

Newer churches have also shown little resistance to formalism at times. For instance, some groups refuse to do critical and background study, insisting on taking the words as they are off the page. Some extreme fundamentalist churches refuse to accept any translation other than the *King James Version*. One sister defended her loyalty to the *King James Version* to me by saying, "If it was good enough for Paul and Peter, it's good enough for me!"

Examples abound; this list could go on for pages. But for now, let's realize that formalism takes the reality out of Scripture and replaces it with repetition and outward readings that have not penetrated into our minds and spirits.

INTERPRETATION: THE FIRST STEP

Some extremist groups believe that studying Scripture is carnal. Consequently, they engage in "prayer reading." They just read verses over and over again while moaning and calling on God to apply the verse. By never discussing the meaning of the passage, they believe they are bypassing the "natural understanding" stage and going directly to the "spiritual understanding" stage.

How wrong this approach is! The Bible is *propositional truth*, which means passages should be understood for their meaning. We have to be prepared to study the context and thought development of each passage we want to understand. We should be able to use language helps to understand vocabulary and grammar. Historical and critical tools available today, even to the English speaker, are fully adequate to interpret all but the most difficult passages.

Finally, we have to consider each passage in the light of our overall understanding of Scripture. If we believe that God has inspired the whole Bible, we should never take statements in isolation, but should consider how they fit into everything the Bible says about that truth. The best protection God has given us against incorrect interpretation is the rest of the Bible.

Every teacher of false doctrine can quote some Bible verses to back up his or her imbalanced position. But those who know the whole counsel of God will quickly see through the misuse of proof texts. There is no shortcut to authentic biblical understanding.

WHERE DO I START?

If we want to experience God's power released through the Bible, we need to accept the importance of personal Bible study (2 Timothy 2:15). How far must we go in studying the Bible to feel secure that we are not unarmed in our struggle? We must at least get to the point where we are *self-starters* in the Word. A self-starter is one who knows how to evaluate most passages in the Bible. A self-starter is able to assess an argument by a Bible teacher, evaluating the value and balance of the argument.

To get this reliable understanding of Scripture, we need to study using sound principles of interpretation. We can learn these principles from books like *How to Read the Bible for All It's Worth* by Gordon Fee or *Protestant Biblical Interpretation* by Bernard Ramm. We will need a modern translation of the Bible so we don't have trouble with the language. We will also need some tools to help us understand the language and the cultural context. A Christian bookstore manager will be able to suggest interesting and helpful Bible study guides.

MEDITATION: THE NEXT STEP

Once we have faithfully done the study and are satisfied with our interpretation of a text, the next step is meditation.

Prayerfully, we ask God to take us deeper into the meaning of the text.

What will happen when we meditate on Scripture? God may immediately shed light on an area of our lives that needs attention. He may show us what we have failed to do in our important relationships or where we have wronged someone and need to change our attitude. He will also encourage us by reminding us of things like His love and answers to prayer.

> *Meditation means we reflect on how a given truth applies to our own or others' lives.*

TRUTH AND EXPERIENCE

Both truth and personal experience are important in the Christian life. However, they are not equal. God says our experience should be understood in light of the truth. For instance, we are told to be anxious for nothing (Philippians 4:6). In other words, when our feelings are telling us to be scared, God says we should overrule our feelings with the truth that He will care for us. The same must be true with the feeling of desire. Desire or thirst for something is a strong emotional experience. But God refers to some desires as "evil" (Colossians 3:5). This is only one of many such statements in Scripture. Unless our thinking is deeply steeped in God's Word, we will often misinterpret our experiences. We need an objective authority by which to judge our feelings, experiences, and circumstances because they are subjective and unreliable.

Have you ever felt as if someone was angry at you, only to find out later that you were wrong? Our feelings and impressions are often in error because our feelings are fallen, just like our thoughts. We can't assume everything we think is automatically right, and neither should we believe everything we feel is necessarily right.

We live in an age that is increasingly losing the distinction between feelings and truth. In our culture, even reality itself has to answer to the feelings and impressions of the individual. The question is no longer "Is it true?" but "Does it work for you?" Though such feelings and impressions may vary from one person to another, that isn't a problem. We just conclude that reality is different for different people! The most important thing, according to the modern world, is to follow our true feelings— to be true to ourselves. The individual and his or her feelings and impressions have thus become the defining center of the universe, the one thing that can never be questioned. The individual's feelings and experience have replaced God, who used to occupy this place.

Today, in addition to the defining role of feelings, we are increasingly confronted with a variety of *mind-power* disciplines. These disciplines aim to train the individual to use his or her mind to change reality. Mind power means, not my ability to learn objective truth, but my ability to project my thoughts outward and impose them on the world. In the modern world, I am not trying to *learn* truth, I am the *source* of truth.

Even in the Christian church, the thinking today is moving more toward the centrality of feelings as the definition of reality. This comes more from the church's tendency to imitate culture than from the Bible. Paul's warning against those who take their stand on visions they have seen (Colossians 2:18) is being ignored.

For all these reasons, we need to cultivate the habit of subjecting our feelings to the scrutiny of the Word of God. Otherwise, we end up undermining the authority of Scripture. Either our feelings and perceptions are *under* the authority of Scripture, or they stand *over* Scripture as the final authority. We must consciously decide which it will be.

Our perceptions and feelings are fallen, just like our behavior. Although modern thinkers want us to "affirm" or "validate" whatever we are feeling, God is not reluctant to rebuke our feelings when they are evil, misguided, or inappropriate. In Nehemiah 8:9, the people were mourning and weeping when Ezra read the Bible to them. But Nehemiah forbade them to grieve or weep, and commanded them to rejoice instead! Their feelings had led them the wrong way in this case. They were corrected by the truth. God's dealings with Jonah contain a similar rebuke for inappropriate feelings.

Maturing in the Lord means learning to distrust our perceptions, at least to the extent of comparing and submitting them to what God says. Refusal to do this constitutes a form of arrogance that can effectively block spiritual growth. If we always think our feelings are the truth, we are not in a position to hear a different point of view from God. We become very headstrong and hard to lead.

Counselors today are worried that Christians will deny or ignore their feelings because they believe such feelings are wrong. This is a valid concern. There is no need to deny or ignore anything. The point is not to deny, but to critique. And we cannot critique our feelings unless we acknowledge them. On the other hand, if we are not prepared to critique our perceptions and feelings, then our feelings have become the true integration point of our lives, rather than God and His Word.

THE BIBLE AND THE OTHER MEANS OF GROWTH

The Word is particularly important in correctly understanding the other means of growth. The following chart details various means of growth and the way in which our use of each is impacted by Scripture. Of course, it is also good to remember that we wouldn't even know about the other means of growth without the Bible.

TABLE 14.1 THE EFFECT OF THE WORD OF GOD ON THE OTHER MEANS OF GROWTH

Means of Growth	Interaction with the Word of God
Prayer	In our prayer life, the Bible provides the proper basis for knowing God by telling us what He is like. According to Jesus, effective prayer is based on the Word (John 15:7). John promises that "if we ask anything according to His will, He hears us. And if we know that He hears us in whatever we ask, we know that we have the requests which we have asked from Him" (1 John 5:14). This is a powerful promise, but it is conditional. We have to ask "according to His will." But how do we know what the will of God is apart from Scripture?
Ministry	Servanthood is a means of growth, but effective service involves "speaking the truth in love" (Ephesians 4:15). No ministry will have the power God wants it to have unless the one ministering is powerful in the Word of God. Even service ministers who may not teach or preach need the wisdom available in God's Word. We will not be effective at ministry or in our personal growth if we cannot fend off the attacks of Satan, and this is not possible unless we are able to cite our authority from Scripture.
Body Life	The basis for Christian fellowship is not only love but truth. The Body of Christ is a community of truth, and these two can never be separated. In Philippians 1:9-10 Paul prays, "that your love may abound still more and more in real knowledge and all discernment, so that you may approve the things that are excellent, in order to be sincere and blameless until the day of Christ." Truth is the framework that makes real love possible. This is why we are called on to "speak the truth in love" to one another (Ephesians 4:15).

Means of Growth	Interaction with the Word of God
Discipline of the Holy Spirit	The discipline of the Holy Spirit is a means of growth, but it won't be effective unless we respond appropriately. We need Scripture like that in Hebrews 12 to teach us how to respond to discipline in a way that promotes growth, as we shall see.

Unless we see all the means of growth as an interconnected plan of provision from God, we will miss God's plan for our lives. The Word of God takes its place at the center of that plan.

CHAPTER 15

WALKING ACCORDING TO THE SPIRIT: FELLOWSHIP

In Christianity, we "set our minds on the things of the Spirit" corporately, not just individually. Many religions offer the option of personal spiritual advancement apart from other people, but not Christianity. As Christians, we are given only one option if we want maturity: spiritual growth in the context of Christian community. God doesn't tell us exactly why He set it up so that we have to depend on others, but He did it. Maybe He didn't want us to become arrogant, thinking we were strong enough in ourselves to grow without others. Maybe He felt we would be safer from the Enemy if we stuck together. Maybe He felt we needed a curb on selfishness. The centrality of love in the Christian ethic accords well with holding fellowship as essential. One thing is clear: God intends Christians to come together as a group regularly so they can grow.

> *Through sharing the common life of Christ with each other in fellowship, we effectively set our minds on the things of the Spirit.*

Christians throughout the New Testament, regardless of locality, are always presented as a community. By assembling together, Christians are able to share the common life of God with one another. This sharing is called *koinonia* in Greek. It is a rich word, often translated "fellowship," but with more meaning than our word *fellowship* conveys. *Koinonia* suggests an exchange of something. It literally means to have in common, or to share. Through sharing the common life of Christ with each other in fellowship, we effectively set our minds on the things of the Spirit.

God has given us spiritual gifts that we can use to build up others. Others can use their gifts to build us up. Therefore, *koinonia*, where we build each other up, is a means of growth. *Koinonia* is a way to set our minds on the things of the Spirit, because it is really God speaking to us through the other members.

An in-depth study of all the passages dealing with the church would be beyond the scope of this book. But if you are not already familiar with basic passages on Christian fellowship, take a minute to study the following chart, which contains some of the relevant biblical data.

TABLE 15.1 FELLOWSHIP AS A MEANS OF GROWTH

1 Corinthians 12:21 And the eye cannot say to the hand, "I have no need of you"; or again the head to the feet, "I have no need of you."	No Christian can claim he or she doesn't need ministry from and to other believers. The context of this statement makes it clear that we have all been given gifts for the edification of others. By implication, if we cannot say we don't need them, they cannot say they don't need us! Notice that it is not just the *presence* of the other members that we need but also their *function*.
1 Corinthians 12:7,14 But to each one is given the manifestation of the Spirit for the common good. . . . For the body is not one member, but many.	Our gifts are for the common good, i.e., for the good of others. Because we are a part, and not the whole, of the Body of Christ, we need what the other parts of the Body supply. God has not gifted any of us so much that we can meet all our own needs.
1 Corinthians 14:26 What is the outcome then, brethren? When you assemble, each one has a psalm, has a teaching, has a revelation, has a tongue, has an interpretation. Let all things be done for edification.	Our times of assembly together are for mutual edification. Whatever you believe about spiritual gifts, there can be no doubt that our meetings are for this purpose. Therefore, if we fail to assemble, we will miss out on edification.

Ephesians 4:15 Speaking the truth in love, we are to grow up in all aspects into Him who is the Head, even Christ.	The Body of Christ should be seen as an organic union based on genuine personal relationships and mutual interdependence. Within these relationships we have the opportunity to speak the truth in love. The important point is not just that we attend meetings (although this is a necessary aspect) but that we authentically share the life of Christ with one another.
Hebrews 10:24-25 Let us consider how to stimulate one another to love and good deeds, not forsaking our own assembling together, as is the habit of some, but encouraging one another; and all the more, as you see the day drawing near.	It is in the context of loving relationships that we can learn to stimulate each other to love and good deeds. Devoting time to our meetings is an essential part of this scenario.
Acts 2:42,46 And they were continually devoting themselves to the apostles' teachings and to fellowship [*Koinonia*], to the breaking of bread and to prayer. . . . And day by day continuing with one mind in the temple, and breaking bread from house to house, they were taking their meals together with gladness and sincerity of heart.	The example of the early Church included extensive involvement in fellowship. This fellowship included both meetings (held at Solomon's portico, which was part of the temple, or in homes) and informal times of social and spiritual relationship building. Their involvement was more or less daily, according to this passage. Real *koinonia* means not just attendance at a meeting or two, but successfully building supportive relationships.
Matthew 18:19-20 Again I say to you, that if two of you agree on earth about anything that they may ask, it shall be done for them by My Father who is in heaven. For where two or three have gathered together in My name, there I am in their midst.	In this passage, Christ puts special emphasis on His presence during times of Christian fellowship. It may be that some prayers will not be answered until we pray "our Father," rather than "my Father."
1 Corinthians 12:18 But now God has placed the members, each one of them, in the body, just as He desired.	The Body of Christ is constituted by God, not by man. A local manifestation of the Body of Christ can take different forms. One of these is an incorporated church. Whether a group is incorporated as a church or not, God recognizes all those who are united with Christ as members of His Body.

Romans 12:4-6 For just as we have many members in one body and all the members do not have the same function, so we, who are many, are one body in Christ, and individually members one of another. And since we have gifts that differ according to the grace given to us, let each exercise them accordingly.	Our identity in Christ includes the aspect that we are also "individually members of one another." This organic, spiritual, or mystical union of believers with Christ and each other is a sacred thing, which should affect our daily lives. We cannot ignore our union with other believers and still live out our new identity in Christ.

BARRIERS TO FELLOWSHIP

Some of us have had negative experiences in churches, and we find it hard to face the prospect of returning to something that hurt or bored us. But we dare not let what wounded us in the past continue to wound us in the present. We have to realize there are different kinds of churches, and if one impacted us negatively, we should look for another.

We in the Western world have an additional barrier to fellowship: the extreme individualism of our culture. Traditional societies see the need for close community much more easily than we do. In our society, Christians often move from city to city or within their own city, resulting in a weakened sense of belonging to any community. Also, extreme individualistic ideology affects everyone in our society. We simply feel we need to go to church only when we get the urge—not because we are an indispensable part of the community. We can minimize the negative impact of radical individualism for ourselves and our families if we choose to view things from God's perspective. This includes prioritizing meaningful involvement in the local church.

FELLOWSHIP UNDER
THE LEGALISTIC PARADIGM

The legalistic mentality sees "going to church" as a religious duty. Failure to observe the Lord's day by not going to church would cause the law-liver to feel guilty. But merely attending church would make this law-oriented person feel good, even though no meaningful *koinonia* may have taken place. Formalism rears its head with fellowship as it does with the other means of growth.

> *To the formalist, the important thing is church membership and attendance at the service. Whether we exchange true ministry with others is unimportant.*

Even when legalists feel obligated to minister in some fashion, the emphasis is on "putting in my time" rather than on Christian love. Many churches still need volunteers, even though they have already relegated most ministry to paid staff. The average Western church has been compared to a football game. Twenty-two men on the field desperately need a rest, while twenty thousand sit in the stands, desperately in need of exercise. The real source of this problem is formalism: the view that the outward institution and schedule of the church is what matters rather than serving others in the name of Christ and building real Christian community.

This is not to say the church does not need organization, or that the outward features of local churches (buildings, pastors, classes, etc.), are not important. The local church must organize ministry if it is to be effective. Church leadership should create structures that facilitate ministry (Ephesians 4:11-12). Also, the church should equip its members for even sophisticated forms of ministry. Once we take the focus off formalistic compliance to a legal standard of attendance and focus instead on the real issue, "faith working through love" (Galatians 5:6), Christian fellowship becomes the means of growth it is supposed to be.

BODY LIFE AND THE OTHER MEANS OF GROWTH
Like all the means of growth, Christian fellowship interacts dynamically with the others. The following chart discusses some of these interactions.

TABLE 15.2 THE INTERACTION OF FELLOWSHIP WITH THE OTHER MEANS OF GROWTH

Prayer	The church is to be a praying community. By precept and example, prayer plays a central role in the life of the church. It is reasonable to think that others can stimulate us to love and good works (Hebrews 10:24-25), including prayer. By establishing regular times to pray with others, we can strengthen our prayer habits, while gaining the discernment of the other members. Prayer is the spearhead of the church's ministry; opening doors, producing conviction in the hearts of those who hear, protecting those reached from Satan, and granting spiritual empowerment to Christian workers.
Ministry	The church exists to accomplish ministry, both to its members and to the world outside the church. Ministry carried out only by myself is never as impactful as that accomplished with others. I need to learn to disciple (train) others so they can carry on the same kind of ministry. I may have to be discipled myself before I can be effective at ministry, and this is best accomplished in a healthy local church.
Scripture	The church should teach the Word of God. The church is ordered to equip its members to do the work of service (Ephesians 4:11-12). Instruction in the Bible is central to this commission.The church should also use the Bible to ground new Christians and even for evangelism at its public meetings.
Discipline of the Holy Spirit	When we are undergoing difficult times of spiritual discipline from the Lord, Christian fellowship is sometimes the only thing that keeps us from falling apart. We were never meant to undergo significant breaking without the support of a loving community. At the same time I receive support, I have the opportunity to give support and to coach young Christians on how to understand God's hand in their lives during trials.

CHAPTER 16

WALKING ACCORDING TO THE SPIRIT: SERVING LOVE

Our beginning point in Romans 8 stressed how essential it is to "set our minds on the things of the Spirit." We can do this through prayer, Bible study, and Christian fellowship, as we have seen. In John 15, Jesus gives us yet another avenue for godly mental focus. He said, "I am the vine, you are the branches; he who abides in Me, and I in him, he bears much fruit; for apart from Me you can do nothing" (verse 5). To abide in Christ includes a Christ-centered mental focus. If we do this, He will bear fruit through us. But some of us have become fruit inspectors. We have lost our focus on the vine and have directed it to the fruit. What a mistake! Fruit is nice, and lack of fruit is unfortunate. But if we want more fruit, our focus should be on the vine, not on the fruit itself.

Jesus went on to further define what He meant by abiding in Him. We have already seen one statement, "If you abide in Me, and My words abide in you, ask whatever you wish, and it shall be done for you." Both the Word and prayer are first on Jesus' list. But His list doesn't stop there.

In verse 9 He also says, "Just as the Father has loved Me, I have also loved you; abide in My love." So abiding in Christ's love is also a part of what it means to abide in the vine. How do we "abide" in the love of Christ? He explains it for us.

"If you keep My commandments, you will abide in My love; just as I have kept My Father's commandments, and abide in His love. . . . This is My commandment, that you love one another, just as I have loved you. Greater love has no one than this, that one lay down his life for his friends." (verses 10-13)

According to this, we abide in the love of Christ when we love one another as He loved us. Keeping Christ's commands (the imperative) is specifically defined, in this passage, as learning how to love others as He has loved us.

When Jesus said "just as I have loved you," He signaled that He is not interested in the purely sentimental modern notion of love. He is more interested in the self-sacrificial love He practiced Himself. Let's compare love as it is understood in the modern world and love as Christ practiced it.

> *This passage, like others, teaches that self-giving love is one important way to set our minds on the things of the Spirit.*

TABLE 16.1 COMPARING BIBLICAL AND MODERN LOVE

Modern Love	Biblical Love
Based on experience—Happens to a person when the "chemistry is right."	Based on a decision—We can decide to invest ourselves in another by giving of ourselves to meet his or her needs. Christ decided to die for us before we even existed (Ephesians 1:3).
Defined by feeling—"I love you" means I feel a certain warmth, desire, or affinity for you.	Compatible with feeling—"I love you" may sometimes mean a feeling, but it always means a commitment to serve. Jesus may not have felt desire or warmth toward the soldiers who flogged Him, but He died for them anyway.
Can't be controlled—Love has to happen, so I can't be expected to choose to love someone. Therefore, love, or lack of love, is not a moral issue.	Can be controlled—Christian love is based on personal choice and commitment. Therefore, it is a moral issue (Mark 12:28-31).

Modern Love	Biblical Love
Depends on the other person—He or she must be attractive or lovely enough to elicit a love response in me.	Depends on God and me—I can love the unlovely, like Christ did when he died for us while we were enemies of God (Romans 5:10).
Self-affirming—Love is a good feeling and must be two-way. If a relationship is not rewarding to me, I have the right to leave and find another.	Self-sacrificial—Christian love is seeking to give victoriously and keeps no record of whether the other person gives back (1 Corinthians 13:5).
Meets others' desires—Effort is extended to please or pacify others by doing what they want.	Meets others' needs—Christian love is concerned with doing what is good for another, not with what the other wants. This love recognizes that what people want and what they need are often different. The other person may need confrontation even if he or she doesn't want it.

LOVING OTHERS EQUALS GROWTH FOR ME

No growing Christian is surprised to discover that God wants us to learn to love others. But how does our giving love tie in with our spiritual growth?

If, by God's grace, we have been successful at building some relationships in our lives, we have the opportunity to practice self-giving love in those relationships. When we do, Christlike love becomes a means of growth. First we come before God and reflect on the needs of our friends and family. Then, using our growing understanding of the Word and ministry, we should lay plans with God to meet those needs, or help them meet their own needs. Both during this planning process and when we carry out our plans, we are setting our minds on the things of the Spirit.

Although we may not notice it right away, we release the power of the Holy Spirit into our lives by thinking of others in an unselfish, spiritual way. We grow through the insights God gives us during times of other-centered reflection and study. But there is much more. The sheer selflessness and Christ-centeredness of our mind-set during these times is spiritually healthy.

Other-centered prayer and reflection bring truth and a closeness to God that often evades us when we merely spend time with God thinking about our own lives.

God is concerned about the spiritual and personal needs of others, and as we selflessly orient our minds this way, we find that we are adopting a perspective similar to God's own. We find ourselves moving the same direction as God, and consequently are better able to move into His thoughts.

Consider just a few of the passages that warn us that serving love is essential for growth.

LOSING MY LIFE FOR THE SAKE OF JESUS

Some Bible teachers worry that Christians will think about their horizontal relationships with other people at the expense of their vertical relationship with God. A "ministry focus," it is argued, could be like Martha cooking dinner for Christ instead of Mary sitting at His feet. This is certainly possible. But it need not be an either/or choice. If we are spending time loving others with real Christian love, depending on Christ as we do so, we *are* abiding in Him, according to the passage we studied earlier (John 15).

Under the impact of spiritual growth, our fundamental life motivation begins to change. Instead of only desiring to receive, we begin to feel the need to give. As we devote mental time and energy to the question of how to build others up, we get outside of ourselves and open a channel of direct blessing from God. The experience of being loved by God transforms us as nothing else can. In a sense, the love of Christ spills over to others.

The fact that we learn to focus on meeting others' needs does not mean we don't have needs of our own or that others can't meet those needs. In fact, it is those who learn to give without looking for return who tend to have their own needs met fully, while those who seek to have their own needs met usually wind up dissatisfied. This is part of what Christ meant in the riddle He shared in Luke 9:24—"For whoever wishes to save his life shall lose it, but whoever loses his life for My sake, he is the one who will save it." When we look away from our own needs for Christ's sake, we will find that He can be trusted to meet those needs better than we ever could through selfish love-demanding. We will be like the Apostle Paul, who was more concerned with other people's problems than with his own.

CODEPENDENT MINISTRY?

Is this codependency? Is this a neurotic servility to others based on unacknowledged love needs of our own? Perhaps. If our serving others is a product of dependency, it could indeed be neurotic. We should not depend on others for our well-being. We should act for *their* well-being. Our positive servitude is not bribery or manipulation—the hope that others will notice how much we have given and show appreciation. If it is, we will not grow as a result. We will be destroyed.

Nothing is worse than setting out on a course of self-sacrifice for the wrong reason, such as an underlying agenda of love taking. A person who serves others for wrong motives looks sacrificial at first. Only later, when the secret expectations go unmet, does the bitterness surface. God, in His grace, will eventually smoke out the one who goes into relationships and ministry for codependent reasons. But we may very well be able to discern the problem before that time.

> *Love-demands chide others for failure to care for me sufficiently. Discipline in love appeals to others to change for their own good.*

The way we practice discipline in love is a key to discerning our motives in the area of dependent, manipulative relating. Are we willing to discipline those we love when they need it? When we speak a word of correction, is it because we are rebuking their failure to meet our expectations, or because such a word is needed in their lives?

Discipline in love is one of the most sacrificial acts possible in a relationship. We have much to lose, because people don't always react maturely. Only when we are determined to act for others' good, not for their appreciation, will we consistently practice godly discipline in relationships.

HAVE SOME DINNER

When His disciples approached after He had been talking to the Samaritan woman, Jesus said, "I have food to eat that you do not know about. . . . My food is to do the will of Him who sent Me, and to accomplish His work" (John 4:32-34). Jesus was being fed spiritually by His encounter with this woman, in which He was able to share the gospel and enrich her life. We, too, can be fed this way. Nothing is more healthy than applying our minds and creativity to the well-being of others, provided we do so in dependence upon God and for the right motives. The Apostle Paul says,

> Do nothing from selfishness or empty conceit, but with humility of mind let each of you regard one another as more important than himself; do not merely look out for your own personal interests, but also for the interests of others. Have this attitude in yourselves which was also in Christ Jesus, who, although He existed in the form of God, did not regard equality with God a thing to be grasped, but emptied Himself. (Philippians 2:3-7)

The Lord wants us to learn to get outside of our own needs and become concerned about meeting the needs of others, just as He did.

Some Christians will argue at this point, "I know I should serve others, and I'm planning to do so, but right now I have a lot of my own problems I'm working through. How can I focus on others' problems when I'm still working through my own?"

In fact, when we are feeling an acute sense of need and hurt, it is more important than ever that we deliberately get outside ourselves, at least part of the time, to meet needs in others. Nothing will help us keep our own problems in perspective more, nothing will give us more motivation, nothing will build our faith more than serving others in the name of Christ. Even in His hour of greatest need the night before His death, Jesus took time to wash the feet of His disciples. Afterward, He told them He had given them an example to follow. Then He said, "If you know these things, you are blessed if you do them" (John 13:17). To be blessed means we will be enriched or happy if we follow His example.

THE MOST IGNORED MEANS OF GROWTH

In theological terms, this act of devoting myself to the project of building relationships where I "edify," or build up, others is called *ministry*. The word for ministry in the Bible is the same as that for service. Anytime we move out in the name of Christ to practice servant love, we are servants, or ministers.

Today, Christian ministry is the most ignored biblical means of growth. In recent years, there seems to be an increasing realization in the church that ministry is important for everyone. However, it is still rarely viewed as a true means of growth, as prayer and Scripture are. In major systematic theologies, serving love often is not even mentioned in the discussion of the means of grace. In a recent popular book on ministry, the author's example of "outreach" was an orderly who hummed hymns on the elevator as he took people to surgery! How far we are from the biblical picture.

Ministry is not seen as a priority sometimes because many churches portray a division between clergy and laypeople. Under this teaching, average Christians often do not view themselves as ministers, because that is a professional role, like dentistry. If your neighbor told you he had a toothache, you would hardly feel competent to take him to your basement shop and drill out his cavity, filling it with epoxy glue! This sort of problem calls for a professional—no layperson should ever try dentistry.

Many have come to view Christian ministry in the same light. They think that the responsibility for ministry belongs to the pastor. Who am I to think I can help people with their problems? How could I build people up spiritually? Unfortunately, modern Christians have lost confidence in their own ability to do sophisticated Christian ministry. But we can do these things, and if we fail to do so, we are missing out on one of the means of growth. No Christian who merely receives blessing from others will ever be healthy spiritually. Many Christians think the reason their churches exist is to meet their needs. How far this is from the biblical picture, where the church is there so we can meet others' needs!

Even though we may advance through the earliest stages of spiritual growth without developing ministry, we will not get very far. Failure to develop ministry is nothing less than a lack of love, and God declares that we cannot move ahead with Him unless we develop meaningful ministry, any more than we could without prayer.

TABLE 16.2 SERVING LOVE—ESSENTIAL FOR GROWTH

Passage	Implication
1 Timothy 1:5 But the goal of our instruction is love from a pure heart and a good conscience and a sincere faith.	If the goal of Paul's instruction is love and the other things mentioned, we would be failing to fulfill that goal apart from ministry.
Ephesians 4:15-16 Speaking the truth in love, we are to grow up in all aspects into Him, who is the head, even Christ, from whom the whole body, being fitted and held together by that which *every joint* supplies, according to the proper working of *each individual part*, causes the growth of the body for the building up of itself in love.	That which builds up the Body of Christ is the power of Christ being ministered to the members ideally through every single individual in that local group. I will grow, not only from receiving blessing from others, but also from giving blessing.
1 John 4:19-20 We love, because He first loved us. If someone says, "I love God," and hates his brother, he is a liar; for *the one who does not love his brother whom he has seen, cannot love God whom he has not seen.*	We might attempt to develop a love for God without bothering to build love for other people. This would be misguided. A Hindu holy man might leave human society to find God through years of spiritual discipline. But a Christian cannot withdraw from others and find a deep walk with God based on personal experience. According to this passage, failure to love others is antithetical to loving God.

Passage	Implication
Acts 20:35 In everything I showed you that by working hard in this manner you must help the weak and remember the words of the Lord Jesus, that He Himself said, "It is more blessed to give than to receive."	The word *blessed* means enriched. We have not experienced most of what God wants to give us in enrichment, including spiritual growth, if we only receive. Financial giving is a part of this picture, but there are other gifts and ministries as well.
John 13:34,17 A new commandment I give to you, that you love one another, even as I have loved you, that you also love one another. If you know these things, you are blessed if you do them.	When Jesus says "these things" the context is His washing of His disciples' feet, a graphic demonstration of servant love. He promises that the one who practices servant love will be more "blessed" as a result, which implies ministry is a means of growth.
Luke 9:24 Whoever wishes to save his life shall lose it, but whoever loses his life for My sake, he is the one who will save it.	This riddle directly opposes modern thinking. It means that those who live for self lose the advantage they sought. It is by denial of self for Christ's sake that we end up being fulfilled.

"I MAY NOT MINISTER, BUT I HAVE THE OTHER MEANS OF GROWTH"

If I have four out of five means of growth, I may conclude that I will be 80 percent healthy. But this is not true. Because of the interaction of the means of growth, missing even one will eventually lead to a sickening distortion of our entire Christian lives.

Because Christian ministry is so often ignored in North America, we have taken the extra step of considering how the *absence* of this means of growth will affect the others. A similar chart could easily be made up for each of the other means, and doing so might be a good idea for personal study. (Refer to table 16.3 on page 168.)

FEEL THE JOY

When Jesus gave His instructions in John 15, He included the statement, "These things I have spoken to you, that My joy may be in you, and that your joy may be made full" (verse 11).

TABLE 16.3 WHEN THE MEANS OF GROWTH ARE ABSENT

Means of Growth	Effect When Ministry Is Absent
Scripture	When we have not developed personal ministry the reason for in-depth study of Scripture is hard to remember. We study only for personal blessing, which eventually leads us to a strictly devotional approach to Scripture. Seriously attacking critical issues seems like a waste of time to Christians who have no defined ministry, because they have not had the experience of being caught without the answers in real ministry situations.
Prayer	Without defined regular ministry in our lives, prayer loses one of its most important forms—intercession. Instead of spending substantial time in intercessory prayer as the New Testament authors did, prayer becomes merely a chance to build myself up. Christians without ministry become increasingly self-centered in prayer, coming to see prayer as a vehicle to transport one into another feeling state, rather than as a tool of spiritual warfare.
Fellowship	When a local church lives in the light of its mission and all the members see themselves as contributing to that mission, a healthy dynamic takes hold. When ministry is not seen as essential for every member, a different dynamic appears. Instead of people having their energies and attention directed outward to the lost and needy of this world, everyone's eyes turn inward. The church becomes corporately self-centered. When a church is inward-focused, in-fighting and dissatisfaction follow soon. People either lose motivation for even the basic operation of the church or begin to seek feeling states and strange experiences in place of ministry. These feeling states become the definition of true spirituality. People's lives remain as immature as ever when they view Christianity as an opportunity for thrill-seeking instead of serving.
Discipline of the Holy Spirit	We may actually avoid some discipline of the Holy Spirit by avoiding ministry. God wants to use our ministry as a tool of discipline in our lives. However, missing out on some of God's discipline in our lives is not a blessing, even though the carnal mentality might think so. Also, as we shall see, the outcome God seeks in discipline is to manifest the life of Christ in our outer persons. This outcome is describing something that enhances our ministries. By failing to develop ministry in our lives we miss the intended outcome of discipline.

Jesus knew that by loving others we would be fulfilling His command and receiving a blessing ourselves while we did it.

Receiving a blessing from God, whether directly from Him or through another Christian, can be pretty exciting. Nothing feels better than the surge of edification we feel sometimes during an anointed Bible teaching or a beautiful spiritual song. There is indeed a place in the Christian life for ecstasy!

But have you ever felt the thrill when the power of the Almighty God moves through *you* to *another* in an act of Christian ministry? If not, you may be missing one of the most important sources of enrichment for Christians. Jesus wasn't kidding when He said, "It is more blessed to give than to receive." The sense of reward is often tangible, not only afterward when the impact of what we have done gradually dawns on us, but even *during* times of Christian service.

HOW DO I START?

If you want to become more involved in Christian ministry but feel uncertain how to proceed, the following points may help.

First, you must be equipped for ministry. This means you have to be trained in the use of the basic tools of Christian ministry. It is your church's job to make training available to you. The Apostle Paul said God gave the church leaders "for the equipping of the saints for the work of service, to the building up of the body of Christ" (Ephesians 4:12). Your church leadership is supposed to provide you with opportunities for training in ministry, or as it reads here, "the work of service."

Next, realize that establishing ministry is different from shining a pair of shoes. Most of us could shine some shoes with little actual training. We could also expect success on our first or second try. Three tries would definitely be adequate for all but the most incompetent. Ministry, on the other hand, is one of the most complicated and sophisticated tasks possible. It also ranks at the top in value and significance. Those who hope to establish meaningful ministry based on a weekend seminar or a couple of attempts at leading a home Bible study are headed for failure. Personal ministry is such a valuable activity, both to ourselves and to others, that we should be prepared to undertake years of training and undergo multiple failures, including some painful ones. There is nothing foolish about suffering intensely in the process of establishing a meaningful ministry. The learning curve extends over years, not weeks.

Let us come before God and adjust our estimates of what is involved in establishing ministry in His name. It is not for us to set limits on what we are prepared to undergo in order to become effective servants of God. If we are setting out on an endeavor that is the will of God, we should be prepared to do whatever He thinks is necessary.

MINISTRY UNDER THE LEGALISTIC PARADIGM

Ministry is as vulnerable to legalism as any other part of the Christian life. Our definition of living under law is that people under law take their identity from what they are doing. When we apply this to ministry, we will find that many of us have fallen under the law paradigm.

Taking our identity from our ministry results in a sickening perversion of God's plan. Results in ministry cause boosts to our ego or devastating personal deflation. Such deflations are not the normal, healthy trials found in all sacrificial service. They are unhealthy because we are overloading our service with a burden it was never meant to bear—our very identity.

Everyone feels bad when things go poorly in ministry. Even the Lord Jesus and Paul felt depressed about the negatives in their ministries. Paul said, after listing a devastating series of trials, "Apart from such external things, there is the daily pressure upon me of concern for all the churches. Who is weak without my being weak? Who is led into sin without my intense concern?" (2 Corinthians 11:28-29). Surely Paul was depressed about ministry at times. Jesus' exasperation was obvious when He cried out, "O unbelieving and perverted generation. . . . How long shall I put up with you?" (Matthew 17:17).

Those who go forward to serve others in the name of the

Lord will encounter staggering negatives from the people they serve. Some of these negatives are so strong they are bound to cause depression and an intense sense of failure.

It is also natural to sometimes feel "burned out" in ministry. Today, many think something is broken if they feel exhausted from ministry work. But even Jesus felt exhausted (John 4:6). Like any other kind of work, ministry can be tiring, and we need times of rest. But when we have been living under a legalistic understanding of ministry for some time, burnout takes the form of defection.

So the question becomes: When are our bad feelings about failure, or our weariness, a sign of legalistic thinking?

Weariness or discouragement over failure indicates legalistic thinking only when our depression causes us to become resentful or unfaithful to the Lord. When we quit ministry because of poor results, it suggests that, perhaps subconsciously, we view success and appreciation from others as preconditions for ministry. In other words, we are not willing to serve if we can't satisfy some inner standard of success and appreciation. Instead of changing tactics or ministry fields, we simply walk off the job. But why should success or recognition be a precondition for going on? Isn't it because we are drawing so much of our identity from our ministry that we cannot tolerate failure without becoming a nobody?

The dividing line is not always easy to detect, because results *are* important. When Paul spoke to the Corinthians about this, he stressed that the harvest was exactly why he and Apollos came to Corinth. They were willing to cooperate with one another because the harvest mattered to God. Therefore Paul could say, "I planted, Apollos watered, but God was causing the growth" (1 Corinthians 3:6). But just because results were important didn't mean they were the basis for Paul's identity. He quickly adds, "So then neither the one who plants nor the one who waters is anything, but God who causes the growth" (verse 7).

Paul's grace perspective was evident, not only in his willingness to acknowledge God as the source of power for his ministry, but also in his willingness to cooperate with Apollos. People with a legalistic mentality compete with their fellow workers and seek recognition from others for their work. Paul was unconcerned about how his success was being reckoned, and he was able to say, "Now he who plants and he who waters are one" (verse 8). Of the fleshly Corinthians, however, he had to ask, "Since there is jealousy and strife among you, are you not fleshly, and are you not walking like mere men?" (verse 3).

A godly attitude in ministry is characterized by two features—the willingness to both acknowledge God as the source of our power and to cooperate with others in humility. When we see the tendency in our own hearts either to quit or to compete, we can fairly ask before God whether we are beginning to slip into a works mentality in our Christian service.

How can we argue that two such different reactions (quitting or competing) are the result of the same legalistic mentality? The difference depends on good or bad results, not different attitudes. No one who has spent a long time in ministry can claim he or she never struggled with this temptation. Again, only the grace of God enables us to lay these attitudes aside and return to Him with empty hands, asking Him to supply us again with His own perspective.

MINISTRY AND THE FAMILY

Our own families are excellent settings for Christian ministry. A friend recently asked me whether my discipleship ministry was as strong as it used to be. I assured him it was. I pointed out that not only was I working with the two men he knew about but that I also had three hot young disciples (learners) at home. We parents need to realize that most of us will not get the chance to lead and disciple our kids when they are grown. Our chance is now, and some of us are missing it.

Our spouses also need our love and ministry. We are often able to meet needs in our spouses' lives that no one else can.

As important as ministry to our own family is, we also need to cultivate ministry opportunities outside our family. Some ask why we can't just minister to our own families. I can suggest two reasons why this is insufficient. First, Jesus challenged us with the thought, "If you love those who love you, what reward have you? Do not even the tax-gatherers do the same?" (Matthew 5:46). Part of self-giving love is the willingness to go outside our comfort zone and initiate love with those who are not interested. Otherwise, the family and even the church can become *corporately selfish*. In other words, we may be giving to others, but by forming a circle and scratching one another's backs, we are doing (as a group) the same thing we criticize the world for—serving only ourselves.

> *Part of self-giving love is the willingness to go outside our comfort zone and initiate love with those who are not interested.*

This leads to a second reason why ministry only inside our families is insufficient. When I try to lead and teach my kids, I do so by modeling the way of life I hope they will follow. Shouldn't my modeling include concern for others outside the home? If not, am I not saying by my actions that my kids are the hub around which the wheel of life revolves? If I devote myself only to them, I am demonstrating a values system that considers only my own children important. They look on and get the wrong message from this—that they are the center of the universe. We may tell them otherwise, but remember, our disciples will usually do what we do, not what we say. We need to show our kids that we prioritize servant love with outsiders while not forgetting our own kids. They will benefit most if our lives are consistent with all that God teaches.

MINISTRY AND THE OTHER MEANS OF GROWTH

Like all the means of growth, ministry is an interactive part of the whole pattern of living God intends for us. We have already seen the negative effect the absence of ministry can have on the other means of growth. Here we consider how ministry will complement the other means in the positive sense.

TABLE 16.4 THE INTERACTION OF MINISTRY AND THE OTHER MEANS OF GROWTH

Scripture	When others are looking to us for guidance and help in their Christian walks there will be a new urgency in our study of Scripture. This is because, as discussed earlier, Scripture holds the key to successful ministry. Feeding young believers the Word of God is basic to most kinds of ministry. Even service-oriented ministry should be carried out in light of the Bible and should include the use of Scripture.
Fellowship	The experience of living in a church that has developed an other-centered perspective and a strong ministry ethic is truly one of the most edifying and exciting experiences possible. It is also one of the most difficult to find. When we have a church which has adopted ministry for all as its ethic, it will equip us and facilitate our ministry through the use of the combined manpower and financial resources in the church. The church becomes the natural place to bring guests and know that others there will not ruin outreach or discipleship efforts, but enhance them.
Prayer	Those who are strong in ministry know how many times their ministries have spurred them on to intense periods of prayer. It is hard for such people to imagine what it would be like to feel the obligation to pray, but without the natural and healthy motivation created by ministry. As ministers, no longer are we merely praying because it's the right thing to do, or because we hope we can feel better as a result. Instead, there are real tasks to accomplish through prayer in the lives of others. Those who are established in defined and personal ministry consistently demonstrate more appreciation for prayer than those who are lacking this vital means of growth.
Discipline of the Holy Spirit	We will see later that spiritual discipline is largely intended to make us more effective in ministy. At the same time being in ministry will cause us to experience maximum benefit from discipline. We regularly find that those who are tied into extensive ministry are prepared and able to endure the necessary suffering to be conformed to the image of Christ for the sake of those people who depend on their ministry. Those who are not active in ministry find it too easy to run in the face of painful discipline.

TWELVE BASKETS

When Jesus had His disciples distribute bread and fish to five thousand people in a miraculous demonstration of His power, they must have been amazed. One gospel says Jesus distributed the food Himself (John 6:11). Another says the disciples did it, but this is no contradiction. God meets the needs of people through human agency much of the time. Therefore, John could fairly say Jesus fed them, even though the disciples passed out the food. And this is a tremendous opportunity for us to be a part of what God is doing. It is possible for God to say either that He is doing it or that we are. Both statements are true.

There is an interesting footnote to the story. After all had eaten their fill, the disciples gathered twelve baskets full of bread and fish. These baskets were twelve in number because they were the personal traveling packs used by the disciples themselves.

Jesus later interpreted this miracle symbolically (John 6:33-35). The bread was symbolic of Himself, coming like manna to meet the needs of the human race. By participating in Christ's work in providing a needed meal for those people, the disciples completed a picture of Christian ministry. They had symbolically taken of Christ and given Him to the people. At the same time the people received a needed meal, the disciples provided themselves with unexpected food for many meals to come. But it would be easy to miss the key to this victory. The disciples were not able to feed five thousand or more people with five loaves and two fish. What they were able to do was place the loaves and fish into Jesus' hands and follow His instructions from there. What they contributed was not *ability* but *availability*.

We, too, may sense our own inadequacy, but we can expect to be fed if we present ourselves to feed others in the name of Jesus.

CHAPTER 17

THE MEANS OF GROWTH: WORKS OR GIFTS?

In Romans 8 Paul taught that we should set our minds on the things of the Spirit, rather than on the things of the flesh. But he also taught in chapter 7 that performance of religious works is not the key to growth. Isn't this a contradiction? Aren't prayer, Bible study, and ministry works? And if they are, isn't it fair to say that spiritual growth is based on works, after all?

As we have seen, if viewed legalistically, these means of growth can indeed be considered works. Under the law paradigm, each of the means of growth is recognized and promoted, but the tone is distorted. But when we view the means of growth correctly, a different picture emerges.

Through the means of growth we reach out our hand to take of the free gift of God's grace and power for spiritual growth. Perhaps an illustration will help.

Suppose you met an eccentric stranger on the street. For no reason he gives you what looks like a cashier's check for the incredible figure of ten million dollars. You can't believe it's authentic, but since the bank it was drawn on is nearby, you decide a one-block walk is not too much effort to find out what the story is.

As you present the check, a sheepish grin on your face, and

explain that you doubt its authenticity, you are stunned to see the teller look up and declare, "This check is legal tender!"

Before she can change her mind, you order it cashed, endorse it, and stride home with a wheelbarrow full of money.

After word gets around, you throw a party to celebrate your amazing fortune. One of your friends stands munching a piece of cake and remarks, "Man, I can't believe you got all that money for doing nothing!"

> *We should not view the means of growth as works, but as the active reception of grace.*

Your head snaps up in surprise. "Wait a minute. I did a lot to get that money! That bank was clear down the street. And what about all that time in line? What about the fact that I endorsed the check? I wouldn't have this money now if I hadn't pulled that pen out and done some serious work!"

What is wrong with this picture?

You would have a point on one level. You had to go to the bank and you had to accept the gift through a process of cooperation with the issuer. But we don't consider this sort of activity "working for a living." All you did was accept a free gift, and that doesn't deserve the name "work."

It's the same way with the means of growth. God has given us several ways to set our minds on the things of the Spirit. When we use these avenues, we are actively receiving grace from Him. We are not working, not as far as God is concerned.

Let's change our illustration a bit so it fits better. Suppose that instead of receiving ten million at once, you merely had to go down to the corner daily and meet the stranger to receive a thousand-dollar check. No matter how many times you go down, he is always there, and he is always good for a grand—sometimes he makes it two thousand.

You may ask, "How many times do I have to go down and meet him?" The best answer would probably be, "How many checks do you want to receive?"

But even this picture is not perfect. Going down to a street corner and meeting strangers is nobody's idea of a good time. To really fit, we would have to devise a story where you received riches while doing something you enjoyed doing anyway. This is the way it is with the means of growth. Although some of us may not initially feel that reading the Bible or praying is our idea of fun, the more we do it, the more fun it becomes. Building good relationships and leading others to Christ would be richly rewarding even if these activities weren't drawing us closer to God. The fact that God has made it possible for us to enjoy genuine accomplishment while also having our mind set on the things of the Spirit is a double blessing.

GOD'S PART AND OUR PART

This is the best way to understand the means of growth. We are obligated to supply certain things from our side as humans, while God supplies the rest from His side. We must supply the willingness to grow. We must decide that we desire to know God more fully and become what He wants us to be. Also, we need to take advantage of the means of growth. Scripture nowhere indicates that God will cause us to grow without these means or that He will cause us to take advantage of these opportunities even if we don't want to. We are expected to come forward and willingly meet God through the means of growth.

If we will not pray, we cannot expect spiritual growth. If we will not open our Bible, we cannot expect to attain maturity spiritually. The same goes for fellowship and serving others in love. Yet, in spite of the fact that some things are required from our side, the Apostle Paul is able to challenge the Galatians with the rhetorical question, "Having begun by the Spirit, are you now being perfected by the flesh?" (Galatians 3:3). We grow in grace not by human effort, but by deciding to come to God through the avenues He has provided.

CHAPTER 18

One Last Means

We have been studying how God nourishes growth in our inner, or spiritual, selves after we meet Christ. But God wants to do more in our lives.

After discussing the building up of our inner person in Romans 8:1-11, the Apostle Paul turns to a second necessary process that we must undertake if we are to be conformed to the image of Christ (verse 29). The next section of Romans 8, verses 12-37, is about suffering and affliction, growth through that suffering, and our attitudes as God allows tribulation to enter our lives. To understand this part, a few simple drawings will help.

In the next series of illustrations, Jesus is pictured as a circle, while we are shown as a square. Passages that say Christ is "in us" could be illustrated simply as a circle inside a square.

But sometimes the picture is a little more complicated. For instance, in John 15:4, Jesus says, "Abide in me, and I in you." This statement reflects both Christ in us and *us in Him*. It is similar to the statements we have been reading in Romans 5–8. It's not only that Christ is in us but that, in our position, we are in Christ. The following illustration pictures both these truths.

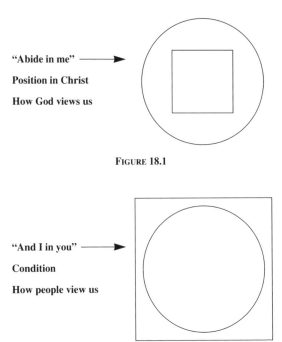

FIGURE 18.1

FIGURE 18.2

In this illustration, the top picture is our *position* in Christ. It reflects frequent statements of Scripture like that in 1 Corinthians 1:30: "By [God's] doing you are in Christ Jesus." The bottom picture illustrates what we have called our *condition* in this life. Just as God looks at us in our position in Christ, others view us in our condition. We also usually view ourselves in our condition, but we have seen that God would like us to view ourselves more in our position, as He does. These two ways of viewing ourselves also explain what has been called the "already–not yet" tension in the New Testament. Both are true of us, depending on how you want to look at it.

As we view ourselves in our position, the power of God is unleashed to build us up spiritually, and a gradual, positive transformation begins.

A MODEL FOR SPIRITUAL GROWTH

Using these symbols, let's picture spiritual growth. Below is an illustration of a new Christian, an adolescent Christian, and a mature Christian. As you can see, the inner spiritual life of Christ is increasingly nourished through the stages. The Spirit is coming to control more of the person's life as he or she matures spiritually.

FIGURE 18.3

But there is something wrong with this picture. Although the inner person is being built up, what is being done about the outer person? My spiritual dimension may be growing closer to God, but my fleshly nature is still there. In Romans 8:10 Paul said, "If Christ is in you, though the body is dead because of sin, yet the spirit is alive because of righteousness." As mentioned earlier, Paul used the term *body* or *flesh* to refer, not just to our physical bodies, but to the whole person we were before we met Christ. The "spirit" refers to the new dimension added after our conversion. Into our deadened selves, God has infused the life of Christ. He nurtures that life through the means of growth we have been discussing. But there is more.

God has introduced a second process that must work alongside the building up of the Christian. This is a destructive process, often described in terms of progressive death. Paul said in Romans 8:13, "If you are living according to the flesh, you must die; but if by the Spirit you are putting to death the deeds of the body, you will live." This process of "putting to death" the deeds of the body, of breaking down the old nature, is the second, destructive process.

A SECOND PROCESS

Our sinful natures inhibit God's ability to express Himself through us. He wants to manifest Himself through us. He wants to use us as instruments of His love for others. To do this, He must find a way through what Paul called our "outer man" (2 Corinthians 4:16), our "flesh" (Romans 8:13), or our "mortal bodies" (Romans 8:11).

When Paul said, "If you are living according to the flesh, you must die," he is not threatening us with physical death if we sin. This "death" is the sense of misery and distance from God that will pervade everything in our lives when we live with a fleshly orientation. Notice that living according to the flesh in this passage is not referring to our life as nonChristians. The passage uses the present tense and describes, not conversion, but a process of spiritual growth when it says "putting to death the deeds of the flesh." This breaking process reduces the rulership of our old natures so that the life of Christ within can show through more clearly. While our inner persons are being built up, our outer persons are being broken down or brought to a place of death.

Paul used the language of life out of death for this process. Just as he said we have died and risen with Christ in our position, here he said we are dying and rising as a process in this life. The difference is clear. Paul consistently referred to our death with Christ as an accomplished fact. But this death is a daily process that never ends. No wonder theologians refer to an "already–not yet" tension in Paul's language.

THE LIFE-OUT-OF-DEATH PROCESS

In one of the clearest passages on the life-out-of-death process, Paul described it this way:

> [We are] always carrying about in the body the dying of
> Jesus, that the life of Jesus also may be manifested in our

body. For we who live are constantly being delivered
over to death for Jesus' sake, that the life of Jesus also
may be manifested in our mortal flesh. (2 Corinthians
4:10-11)

Later in the same passage, he restated it this way: "Therefore
we do not lose heart, but though our outer man is decaying, yet
our inner man is being renewed day by day" (4:16).

At the same time our inner persons are being built up, there
is a "decaying" or a "carrying about in the body the dying of
Jesus." Life springs out of death according to these statements,
just as Jesus spoke of His own mission as being one of bringing
life out of death (John 12:24-26).

How does this death, or decaying process, work? What
does it mean to "by the Spirit . . . [put] to death the deeds of the
flesh"? These are the questions we will seek to answer in the next
chapter.

CHAPTER 19

LIFE OUT OF DEATH

We have seen that there is both a constructive and a destructive process at work in our lives. While we cooperate with God on building up our inner spiritual person, He goes to work on our outer person, seeking to break its stranglehold on us. The Apostle Paul says the reason God has to break down the outer person is so the inner person, or what he calls the "life of Jesus," can be "manifested in our body" (2 Corinthians 4:10).

What does the word *manifest* mean? It means to show, to reveal, or to demonstrate. God wants to show Himself through us, but something is preventing Him. Our outer person continues to express us, not Christ.

The notion that Christ is being manifested through us leads to another of Paul's statements in 2 Corinthians 4:12—"So death works in us, but life in you." Here is the principle of Christian service, or ministry. The Body of Christ is fed when some of its members cooperate with God's work of putting to death the deeds of the flesh in their lives. Why can some people bless us so powerfully when they minister to us? It is more than just years of study and prayer that gives them this ability. It is also the maturing action of the Spirit, including suffering in their lives. We who want to count for Christ must accept that this will only be possible if we are prepared to bear in our body the death of Jesus.

WHAT BREAKS THE FLESH?

God uses things like Scripture, prayer, fellowship, and ministry to build up the inner person. But these things won't work on the outer person. According to 1 Corinthians 2:14, "A natural man does not accept the things of the Spirit of God; for they are foolishness to him, and he cannot understand them, because they are spiritually appraised."

We can read the Bible to our flesh nature all night without the slightest effect! The flesh may even learn how to pray and be a bold voice at prayer meetings. But spiritual things like these sail through the flesh without effect. So what will God use to break down our flesh nature?

For this work, God uses outward experience and circumstances. Just as spiritual things affect the inner person, outward things affect the flesh. Things like affliction, illness, persecution, failure, or danger are like blows upon the hard shell of the flesh. Potentially, we could see a crack forced through the shell, preventing the manifestation of Christ through us, as the following set of illustrations suggests.

> *If we want the life of Christ to be manifested through us, we will have to submit to a painful but necessary process of gradual death in our outer person. True spiritual effectiveness in Christian ministry is predicated upon our brokenness and conformity to the image of Christ.*

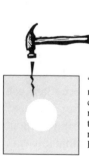

"I'm sick of my roommates," whines the college student. "I'm not going to live with their selfishness and rudeness anymore. I'm getting married!"

"Marriage isn't as easy as I thought it would be."

Figure 19.1

As these cracks widen, more and more of Christ could be manifested through us, as the following illustration shows.

A MORE COMPLETE MODEL

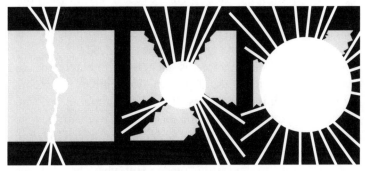

FIGURE 19.2

In this illustration, there is both the building up of the inner person and the breaking down of the outer person. The result is an increasingly powerful manifestation of the life of Christ. Even the young Christian, symbolized on the left, may have fissures through which God is able to manifest Himself. These become gaping holes in the adolescent Christian. But even the most mature Christian, symbolized on the right, will still have some features of the flesh clinging to his or her nature.

HOW WILL GOD DO IT?

Paul mentioned some ominous experiences in connection with the breaking work of the Holy Spirit. In Romans 8:36 he said, "For Thy sake, we are being put to death all day long." In another passage he said, "We are afflicted in every way, but not crushed; perplexed, but not despairing; persecuted, but not forsaken; struck down, but not destroyed" (2 Corinthians 4:8-9). What does it mean to be afflicted in every way? To be struck down? To be perplexed or persecuted?

The heart of sin is autonomy, or self-sufficiency. God may use virtually any kind of suffering experience to strike blows at this self-sufficiency. As we face failure, suffering, and pain, we are thrown back into dependence upon God in a new way. Sometimes only the most acute despair will finally force us to abandon hope in the self life. In 2 Corinthians 1:8-9, Paul recounted that "we were burdened excessively, beyond our strength, so that we despaired even of life; indeed, we had the sentence of death within ourselves in order that we should not trust in ourselves, but in God who raises the dead."

Part of the process before us, then, is the unhinging of our confidence in the fleshly strategies we have employed for coping with problems in our lives. If Paul's example in 2 Corinthians 1 is typical, only affliction that is excessive and "beyond our strength" (that is, our natural strength apart from God) will be sufficient to accomplish what God has in mind. This description is ominous to the serious reader. But what choice do we have? Either we submit to God's plan for our lives, or we strike out on our own and devise a worse fate for ourselves. Paul was glad he had gone through this experience, and no doubt we will be, too, if we endure it.

CONFORMED TO THE IMAGE OF CHRIST
In Romans 8:28-29 Paul discussed the big picture:

> We know that God causes all things to work together for good to those who love God, to those who are called according to His purpose. For whom He foreknew, He also predestined to become conformed to the image of His Son, that He might be the first-born among many brethren.

People like to quote part of this verse at funerals and other tragic events. Usually, the formula goes, "All things work together for good." In this form, it sounds like a sort of mindless positive fatalism. But that isn't what the verse says. The verse makes an important promise, but there are also important conditions and restrictions on the promise.

First, God never says in this verse that He is the One who

causes all things. He rather says He works all things together for good under certain circumstances. In other words, in a fallen world, He has plenty of suffering experiences to choose from, and He need not be the cause of such experiences in any direct sense. Job's friends got into trouble in the Old Testament epic for speculating that God had been the cause of Job's suffering, going so far as to arrogantly claim they knew the reason for Job's disaster. In fact, they knew almost nothing. The direct cause of Job's suffering was the Devil, and their attempts to put God into a cause-and-effect box were superstitious and cruel to Job.

Second, this verse does not claim that God works all things together for good. It says He only works things together for the good of *certain people*; namely, *those who love Him and are called according to His purpose*. To those people, and only to those people, everything will be used by God for good. The description seems to include not even all Christians, although some would argue this point. In the view of most, only those Christians who have fully accepted the prospect of unqualified spiritual growth can rely on this promise.

> *God wants me to become more Christlike in this life, and when I am cooperating with that purpose, every circumstance will serve to further me along the way.*

Finally, what "purpose" do we have to be called to, and what does it mean to have things "work together for good"?

The next verse explains the purpose. "For whom He foreknew, He also predestined to become conformed to the image of His Son, that He might be the first-born among many brethren" (Romans 8:29). The connecting word *for* means this verse continues the thought from the previous verse. The purpose of God is that we be "conformed to the image of His Son." This is the "good" to which God will work all things.

IS THIS ASCETICISM?

If we love God, and if we have accepted that His purpose for us is the best, He will set about the work of conforming us to the image of His Son. This process will include both a building up of the inner person and a breaking down of the outer person.

In other words, if we are planning to follow God, we are going to suffer.

Many religious types focus on suffering to an extraordinary degree. Not only in Christianity but in most world religions there are those who believe that suffering is good for spiritual development, even to the point where they inflict serious punishment upon themselves. Some deprive themselves of normal pleasures. Others stab, cut, beat, and otherwise torment their bodies. These practitioners are usually lumped together under the term *ascetics*. Ascetics are people who believe that suffering is the key to spiritual growth or enlightenment, even when it is self-inflicted. They usually want to punish the body or suppress it through tormenting it into submission.

Critics have claimed that Paul was an ascetic, but he was not. Asceticism is alien to the Bible. Paul says these theories are based on human religious speculation and are worthless. For instance, in Colossians 2:20-23 he says,

> If you have died with Christ to the elementary principles of the world, why, as if you were living in the world, do you submit yourself to decrees, such as, "Do not handle, do not taste, do not touch!" (which all refer to things destined to perish with the using)—in accordance with the commandments and teachings of men? These are matters which have, to be sure, the appearance of wisdom in self-made religion and self-abasement and severe treatment of the body, but are of no value against fleshly indulgence.

We see here that things like abstinence from normal appetites and severe treatment of the body are worthless against fleshly indulgence. Indeed, if we properly understand these superstitious notions, we will realize that they themselves *are* fleshly indulgences. Religious fleshliness is the worst kind, and Jesus reserved His harshest rebukes for religious people (Matthew 23).

Our verses about bearing the dying of Jesus in our flesh are completely different from the ascetic ideal. For one thing, we never need to intentionally inflict suffering upon ourselves. God is merely warning us that He will permit suffering to enter our lives. He is not instructing us to seek suffering.

Second, our suffering is not an end in itself, but a means to an end. When Paul says in one passage, "Therefore I run in such a way, as not without aim; I box in such a way, as not beating the air; but I buffet my body and make it my slave, lest possibly, after I have preached to others, I myself should be disqualified" (1 Corinthians 9:26-27), he is speaking in the context of athletic conditioning. His "buffeting [his] body" is metaphorical, referring to the kind of discipline athletes exercise when they train for their events. Specifically he says, "For though I am free from all men, I have made myself a slave to all, that I might win the more" (1 Corinthians 9:19). This is not asceticism, where pain is an end in itself. Pain endured in the pursuit of a goal is pragmatic suffering. Asceticism seeks pain for nonpragmatic reasons, such as inner enlightenment.

The emphasis in all biblical passages about suffering is not to seek it, as though it were a virtue, but to endure it with the right attitude. We should never turn away from a course that is God's will just because it may involve suffering. But neither should we be suspicious when God leads us into a period of pleasure. God is not interested in seeing us suffer unless it is necessary for our growth. We can let Him decide when that is the case.

DISCIPLINE OF THE HOLY SPIRIT UNDER THE LEGALISTIC PARADIGM

Those who draw their identity from their works will distort the doctrine of the Holy Spirit's discipline. Asceticism is one possibility for legalistic thinkers, and we have already seen why asceticism has no place in biblical Christianity. Most ascetics are indeed very legalistic.

However, there is another, far more common distortion seen in legalistic thinking. This distortion confuses spiritual discipline with justice, even though there is no connection between the two. The following chart helps us understand the difference between these two concepts.

TABLE 19.1 JUSTICE COMPARED TO DISCIPLINE

Justice	Discipline
Because of His justice, God will pay back evil with punishment that fits the crime. This is the doctrine of hell. Justice also rewards good.	Under discipline, there is no matching of a given behavior with a corresponding punishment or reward. Instead, the focus is on what will benefit the recipient.
All human beings fall short of the minimum standard of good under God's justice. All are deserving of judgment. Christians believe judgment was carried out on Christ.	Under discipline, the recipient is the object of love. Since the goal is the betterment of the recipient, discipline is related to conditions in the person's life, not to acts of wrongdoing per se.
Justice looks to the past to ascertain whether the punishment fits the crime.	Discipline looks toward the future to determine whether the actions will help the recipient improve.
Justice cannot refuse to punish one who deserves it.	Discipline is free to react to any action in the way that will be most beneficial to the recipient. This could include doing nothing in some situations.
Justice would never act to punish one who has done no wrong.	Discipline may bring suffering into the life of one who has done no particular wrong. The larger picture of the development of the person's life means breaking may be necessary even though there have been no outstanding problems lately.

You can see from this chart that judgment and discipline are not the same or even similar. A proper understanding of discipline will lead us away from asking questions like "Why is God punishing me?" While we would never want to rule out God's freedom to inflict discipline in connection with specific behaviors, the fact is that discipline is often not directly connected to a specific sin or group of sins. Instead, God is often working on our lives in a more general way.

The person who speculates about whether God let his car break down to get back at him for losing his temper is usually headed the wrong way. This sort of speculation is related more to justice and legalism than it is to discipline. Paul is aware of our tendency to interpret discipline legalistically. In Romans 8:33 he wrote, "Who will bring a charge against God's elect? God is the one who justifies." In the context of the sanctifying effect of suffering on believers' lives, Paul reminds us that such accusations should be ignored.

The fact is, legalists have a hard time understanding discipline, because it is so nonlegalistic. We commonly see two paradoxical reactions from legalistic thinkers regarding the need to discipline those we love. On one hand there will sometimes be a wooden harshness that insists punishment must fit the crime. Leniency will be seen as a betrayal of God's standards. On other occasions legalists will express horror at the idea of disciplining someone. They may charge that if we discipline, we are rejecting or being unloving to the recipient. Ironically, both of these antithetical views arise from the same ideological font: legalism. Let's see how they work and why they are both wrong.

"Punishment Must Fit the Crime"

Under discipline there is no need to make the consequence fit the crime. Any sense that we must do so is a justice argument, which is legalistic. Under discipline the point is not to fit the crime but to help the recipient. Perhaps we can see this better if we speak in terms of child rearing.

I might elect to discipline one child for wrongdoing while doing nothing to another for a similar wrong. My reasons might have to do with the recent history of discipline for both children, the state of their relationship with me, their morale or confidence with regard to behavior, and their temperament or age, among other things. The main thing would be to determine what will do the most good. Of course, if my kids have anything to say about it, they will probably try to get me into some legalistic hammerlock of obligation. "You didn't do this to so-and-so when he did the same thing!" Hopefully, because of my understanding of the freedom we have in disciplinary situations, I won't let them box me in this way.

God has this same freedom when dealing with us. He will guide us into experiences suited to our growth, not matched to our past sins. We also have the important promise that He will not let us undergo any trial we are not able to endure (1 Corinthians 10:13).

"Discipline Is Rejection or Lack of Love"

This thought follows from the mistaken connection between discipline and judgment. Judgment *is* antithetical to love, as can be seen from the fact that those in hell will never experience the love of God. They have been rejected in the truest sense. Likewise, a judge who bent the law for one he loved would be "unjust." Thus it is easy to see why legalists often feel that discipline is rejection. They are really thinking (without knowing it) that judgment is rejection.

Legalistic individuals—whether they lean toward the rigid application of discipline or resist all discipline—are usually expressing their legalism in accordance with their temperamental leanings. Also, the same legalist may swing from one extreme to another at different times and with different people, usually depending on whether judgment or manipulation is the goal in that particular relationship. The sad thing for all legalists, however, is that those they love miss out on the benefits of loving discipline.

In the legalist's own life problems develop because the same faulty definitions are applied when God tries to discipline the legalist. Legalists either feel rejected by God or live in fear and anticipation that God is going to get them back for something they did. Neither fate awaits them, but such faulty expectations can poison their relationship with the Lord.

THE GRACE PERSPECTIVE

When we think God's discipline is always a cause-and-effect reaction to specific sins we have committed, our attention is diverted to our actions as the key to avoiding divine "anger." Instead, we should be looking to what God is trying to do in love through letting us encounter trials. Increasingly, those growing under the grace of God come to view His disciplining hand as a mark of His love and care. We are able to look toward God, trusting that He will work appropriately.

CHAPTER 20

CONDITIONS FOR LIFE
OUT OF DEATH

The suffering God allows to enter our lives will not necessarily conform us to the image of Christ. Have you ever wondered why it is necessary for us to understand what God is doing as He allows us to bear in our body the dying of Jesus? Can't He just do it, and leave it at that? The answer is no.

Here is another question: Why do some Christians seem to suffer without growing? Won't all Christians who suffer grow in proportion to their suffering? Again, the answer is no. Certain conditions must be present from our side before we can expect to see our suffering conform us to the image of Christ.

CONDITION 1: ACTIVE COOPERATIVE FAITH
God is looking for active, conscious cooperation from us as He transforms our lives. Passive assent is never enough. We have to step forward, adopting the right attitude, and seek to know what specific insights He is trying to show us in each situation. We have to willingly acknowledge that the hand of God is shaping us, not just sociological or physical factors.

We will know we have the right attitude when we are able to thank God in the midst of trials. God says, "In everything give thanks" (1 Thessalonians 5:18). Notice, He does not say,

"*For* everything give thanks." Some things are atrocities. Some things are tragic. We are not thankful for those things, as though God committed the atrocity. Instead, He says, "*In* everything give thanks." This means we should understand that even in the worst circumstance, God has a way to turn it to our account. Our trust in God's promises enables us to thank Him for what we know will be the eventual outcome.

Quadriplegic Christian artist Joni Eareckson Tada has testified that she is now glad for the accident that left her handicapped. Few of us will be asked to undergo this particular form of suffering, but we will be asked to undergo some form of suffering—often more than we expected. Paul said, "'We were considered as sheep to be slaughtered.' But in all these things we overwhelmingly conquer through Him who loved us" (Romans 8:36-37). God is seeking this attitude. When we are too spiritually blind to see His hand in our circumstances, we live in a world of fleshly resentment instead of spiritual thanksgiving.

CONDITION 2: SUFFERING IS NOT THE RESULT OF SIN

To state this condition more accurately and carefully: Our suffering should usually not be the result of personal sin on our part, including sins of omission.

The Apostle Peter warned us, "By no means let any of you suffer as [an] . . . evildoer" (1 Peter 4:15). When Christians use heroin, they become addicted just like nonChristians. When we break the law, we go to jail just like nonChristians. When we stick our hand in a fire, we get burned like everyone else. If our suffer-

> *Our suffering should usually not be the result of personal sin on our part, including sins of omission.*

ing is the direct result of something we are doing wrong, the biblical response would be to change what we are doing. It would be a mistake to passively thank God for a situation that is not His will.

Some suffering is not God's will and will not help us grow. If I feel the pain of loneliness because I always come home from work and sit by myself, God would have me rise up, go out to where other people are, and try to establish relationships. I cannot sit in such loneliness waiting for God to transform me through it, because this pain is outside the will of God in the first place. God could use this pain to raise the need level in my life, but unless I respond by changing I will eventually bring further growth to a halt. God wants me to step forward, trusting Him to supply the opportunity and power, and place myself in a position where He can teach me how to relate to others.

Strangely, God sometimes does bless us through suffering we have brought on ourselves by sinning, but not always. For instance, an alcoholic who will not take steps with his drinking will sometimes go for years without spiritual growth. Yet, if we are honest, we must conclude that much of our suffering is connected in some way to our personal sin, and God often uses our own sin to bless us.

The Bible has examples of this kind of blessing. For instance, God was not happy when the Israelites demanded a king during the period of the judges (1 Samuel 8:5-7). He said this was really a rejection of Him as their king. Yet, He allowed them to do it, and eventually He declared that the dynasty they created would culminate in the ultimate king—King Messiah! On another occasion, David committed adultery and murder in order to get Bathsheba as his wife. God disciplined him, but He also used Bathsheba to bring forth the line of the Messiah.

God can definitely bring good out of evil. However, He is not obligated to do so, and He may determine that the best response to sin in our lives is to let us "stew in our own juices" until we are sick of a certain ungodly way of life. This could be viewed as a form of corrective discipline. God has made it clear that His will is that disciplinary suffering not be the result of our own sin.

For this reason, we are better off when we try to avoid damaging sins of commission or omission—not because the presence or absence of these things constitutes spiritual growth, or even because it guarantees spiritual growth. We should avoid such things because:

- ♦ It is the will of God, who loves us and has given Himself up for us.
- ♦ The consequences of sin in this life could be severe.
- ♦ Many sins harm those we want to bless.

This goes back to our earlier discussion of the common cold. There is nothing wrong with limiting or reducing the symptoms of a cold, even though this is not a cure. While we are waiting on the Lord for maturity, we should seek to limit serious sin, *even by outward constraints*, so that we will not be interfering with God's plan for our growth.

CONDITION 3: NO ILLEGITIMATE PAIN REDUCERS

We all have ways to avoid pain. Maybe we withdraw to avoid relational pain, or we may drink or eat when we are depressed. Maybe we rage and shout when people get too close, or we run into another sex experience or even embark upon a spending spree when we're lonely. We all have ways to avoid pain. These strategies give rise to a number of problems when God is trying to work on our outer person. One problem is that many of these strategies involve something overtly immoral. Others are not overtly immoral. Spending money or eating food is not a sin. But when these become illegitimate pain reducers, there is another problem.

> *Our pain-reduction strategies become, in essence, a rip cord we pull whenever our pain reaches a certain threshold.*

If God brings us to a point of personal pain in our lives, it is for our good. If there were a way to accomplish His ends without pain, we can be sure He would do it. But if we jerk the rip cord just before we learn why we came to that point, we effectively short-circuit the work of God.

It isn't easy to teach your child to ride a bike. The child pedals around on training wheels for a few weeks and gains the feeling that he or she knows how to do it. But, of course, the child doesn't know how to balance the bike. Every time the child loses his or her balance, the training wheels save the child from pain. To really learn to ride a bike, the child must take off the training wheels. The trainer has to watch the child fall and usually get hurt. What other way is there?

We must be prepared to experience pain without the training wheels we have been using in our lives. Otherwise, we will never make it to the point where the dying of Jesus is effectively borne in our outer person. We must reject the use of illegitimate pain reducers.

In Hebrews 12 God discusses the problem of losing our composure under the hand of His discipline:

> All discipline for the moment seems not to be joyful, but
> sorrowful; yet to those who have been trained by it,
> afterwards it yields the peaceful fruit of righteousness.
> Therefore, strengthen the hands that are weak and the
> knees that are feeble, and make straight paths for your
> feet, so that the limb which is lame may not be put out
> of joint, but rather be healed. (12:11-13)

All discipline is not enjoyable, but it works. The most interesting phrase in this passage is the last one. What does it mean when He warns that "the limb which is lame may not be put out of joint, but be healed"?

In the ancient world, breaking a bone could be a life-threatening experience. The ancients knew how to set some broken bones and how to relocate some dislocated joints. However, they didn't know much about anesthesia. Imagine breaking your leg and facing the prospect of an ancient doctor setting your bone without any anesthesia! The operation of setting a bone is one of the most painful experiences known to humans. Yet, it was essential that one who had broken a bone hold still while the doctor worked. If the injured person thrashed about in pain, he or she could dislocate the fracture even more, possibly to the point where the doctor could no longer set the bone. There were people hobbling around the ancient world on crutches for life because they had simply broken a leg once. In their case the lame limb was put completely out of joint.

It is no exaggeration to say that, in the ancient world, your future might depend on your ability to hold still and let the doctor work. This is the real-life circumstance that the author of Hebrews chose to illustrate our need to hold still and let God work. When he told his readers to "make straight paths" for their feet, he was urging them to resist the temptation to flee from the disciplining hand of God into their artificial pain reducers. The stakes are very high. We have the opportunity to grow into authentic maturity in Christ, but only if we hold still and let the Doctor work!

We dare not simply flee relationships when they get too painful. We dare not desert the role of service God has given us in the church every time we feel bad or fail to see the results we were looking for. If we won't hold still for God, we might effectively stall the work of God in our lives by fleeing every time God corners our flesh.

A Qualification

We should reject the use of illegitimate pain reducers. However, there is no need to turn away from *legitimate* means of reducing pain in our lives. If we have a headache, we should feel free to take aspirin. If we are tired, we should feel free to sleep an appropriate amount. If we are feeling too much stress, there is nothing wrong with taking a vacation. Any refusal to use reasonable means available to us, provided they are not sinful, would suggest asceticism. It would suggest that we enjoy pain or think pain is good in its own right.

Even changing our circumstances may be in order. If certain circumstances are intolerable, changing them may be the only wise solution. A lousy job may not be worth keeping, especially when a better job is offered. A classic case would be when a Christian wife faces a drunk and violent husband who abuses her and the children. Some situations need to be changed before we can expect to succeed in working with them.

A legalistic mentality would insist we spell out which are legitimate and which are illegitimate pain reducers. But we know better than that. This is not a legalistic principle. God will have to show us when a given activity is becoming harmful to His plan for breaking our outward persons.

CONDITION 4: A POSITION-ORIENTED PERSPECTIVE
In both of our passages on the life-out-of-death process, the Apostle Paul referred to his own perspective on life as he is in the midst of trials. In 2 Corinthians 4 he put it this way:

> Therefore we do not lose heart, but though our outer man is decaying, yet our inner man is being renewed day by day. For momentary, light affliction is producing for us an eternal weight of glory far beyond all comparison, *while we look not at the things which are seen, but at the things which are not seen;* for the things which are seen are temporal, but the things which are not seen are eternal. (verses 16-18, emphasis added)

Here we see what we are to do while God works. Strangely, Paul seems to say we should *look away* from the process of breaking down and building up, even while we go through it, just as we would look away while the doctor sets our broken leg.

We are not to focus on whether our flesh has borne sufficiently the dying of Jesus, or whether we have yet manifested the life of Christ in proper measure. We

We should look away from the breaking process and toward our position in Christ.

are to look away from our condition altogether and focus on our position (or new identity) in Christ. We trust Him to complete the process of life out of death, without constantly monitoring His progress.

We have already seen that if we constantly take our spiritual temperature, we become like spiritual hypochondriacs. I don't worry about whether I have a cold or some other physical disease unless I am presented with some objective, unusual symptoms. If my focus is on my physical health all the time, it takes away from my effectiveness in every area. Some people even become incapacitated by focusing on their ailments. Likewise, in the spiritual realm, we need to set our minds on what we already are in Christ (the unseen), not on what we have become so far in our condition in this life (what is seen). We cannot sit around trying to measure our growth without developing a performance-oriented perspective, and we have seen the problems with that outlook.

Instead, we are to, in a sense, look away from our current progress and move forward, focusing on the things of the Spirit. In Romans 8 Paul says, in the midst of his discussion about God bringing life out of death in our present lives,

> The Spirit Himself bears witness with our spirit that we are children of God, and if children, heirs also, heirs of God and fellow heirs with Christ, if indeed we suffer with Him in order that we may also be glorified with Him. (Romans 8:16-17)

Why discuss our inheritance in the Kingdom of God in the middle of a passage about spiritual growth? By focusing on our future high status, we gain the courage to endure suffering in this life. Notice how similar the next verse is to the one we saw earlier in 2 Corinthians 4:18. "For I consider that the sufferings of this present time are not worthy to be compared with the glory that is to be revealed to us" (Romans 8:18).

Only those who know where they are

Only those who know where they are headed eternally can be expected to welcome suffering.

headed eternally can be expected to welcome suffering. We have the security of future wealth and well-being, and this is why we are willing to suffer in this life for a time.

No wonder Paul seems to digress into eschatology (the doctrine of the end things, like Heaven) in the middle of a discussion about spiritual growth. We have to look back to what Christ has already done and look ahead to what He is going to do before we will be likely to trust Him now as He leads us through both pleasant and unpleasant experiences.

CHAPTER 21

HOW IT ALL ADDS UP

Romans 8:29 promises us as Christians the opportunity to be conformed to the image of Christ. What does this mean? What would we be like if we underwent this growth process?

We have spoken of spiritual growth in the abstract and have analyzed its parts. Our study has also generally centered in the book of Romans, chapters 5–8, and parallels. But it is particularly helpful at times to consider the pattern God has in mind for us by using a real model of Christian living. At this point, we will leave Romans for a look at what sort of person the author of Romans became after many years of spiritual growth. Perhaps by examining a snapshot of a mature Christian, we can get the big picture of what kind of people God wants us to become.

Although the New Testament provides biographical information on apostles Paul, Peter, and John in their later lives, by far most of the detailed material is on Paul. When Paul wrote the Prison Epistles (Ephesians, Philippians, Colossians, and Philemon), he had been a walking Christian for well over twenty years. When he wrote the Pastoral Epistles (1 and 2 Timothy and Titus), he was probably older yet. What sort of person is revealed in this literature?

In order to keep our study short, we will focus on the book

of Philippians and refer to some of the other books when they bear on our subject in a special way. Philippians contains some of the most interesting material because it is addressed to one of Paul's favorite groups and was written in the face of the gravest of trials.

THE SETTING
The book of Philippians, like the other so-called Prison Epistles, was written during the two years mentioned at the end of Acts 28. This passage describes the period after Paul's arrest in Judea and his transport as a prisoner to Rome for trial. Luke wrote, "When we entered Rome, Paul was allowed to stay by himself, with the soldier who was guarding him" (Acts 28:16). We read in verses 30-31, "He stayed two full years in his own rented quarters, and was welcoming all who came to him, preaching the kingdom of God, and teaching concerning the Lord Jesus Christ with all openness, unhindered."

From Philippians 1 we can determine that Paul was facing possible death at the hands of the Romans when he wrote. The charges against him, which included sedition and incitement to riot, often carried the death penalty, and his hearing with Caesar's court must have been imminent. Philippians 1:20-23 and 2:17 make it clear that Paul was contemplating the possibility of his own death.

WHY IS THIS MAN IN JAIL?
At this time, Paul was probably the most competent and experienced Christian church planter in the world. It must have been terribly difficult for a man of action, training, and competence, like Paul, to understand God's reasons for leaving him in prison, first in Palestine, and then in Rome.

As we discussed earlier, serious Christians should develop the habit of always asking what God is trying to do through our trials. This ability to look at our problems from the perspective of what God is doing is what we have called the "vertical perspective." Paul had this perspective, clearly seen in Philippians

1:12-13—"Now I want you to know, brothers, that what has happened to me has really served to advance the gospel. As a result, it has become clear throughout the whole palace guard and to everyone else that I am in chains for Christ" (NIV). Amazingly, Paul saw his imprisonment as furthering the work of God.

Imagine Paul turning to God with the painful question of why he had been left in jail, only to look down to his manacled wrist. His eyes follow the chain attached to his manacle until it ends—fastened to the wrist of his private Roman guard. A smile slowly spreads over Paul's face. "Hi!" he says, as he warms to another opportunity to share the truth about Jesus Christ. The Roman soldier chained to Paul's arm probably believed he had his prisoner securely locked in place. Paul felt the soldier was *his* prisoner!

The palace guard, or praetorian guard, refers to a Roman legion of around seven thousand men in or near Rome. They were an elite corps who would have been very influential. Even if the term "whole palace guard" is hyperbole, it is a remarkable statement.

We know from studies of the early Church that Christianity was spread in part by retiring soldiers, who, after their service to the state, were often given a piece of land in one of the provinces. Who would have guessed that God had Paul chained to men who after listening to a complete, carefully reasoned presentation of the gospel every day, would spread Christianity throughout this elite group of Roman citizens, and from there, throughout the empire? Paul knew something we should remember:

> *When suffering trials, God is often prepared to accomplish goals through us if we will only adopt the right point of view.*

It is clear that Paul immediately looked for God's purpose in his circumstances. In fact, he manifests this vertical attitude—looking at things from God's viewpoint rather than man's—in every area he touches. I think this vertical attitude is the most striking thing about Paul in his later years.

Paul often goes so far as to call himself the prisoner of the Lord (Ephesians 3:1, 4:1; 2 Timothy 1:8; Philemon 1,9). How completely he had adopted the vertical perspective! He no longer acknowledged humans as the ones holding him prisoner. If he was a prisoner (and, of course, the reason for his imprisonment was his witness for Christ, not any wrongdoing), it was because God had him there for His own purposes. With such an expectant faith, Paul was in a position to make the most out of a situation that must have seemed absurd on the horizontal level.

With scores of local churches yearning for a visit from Paul, not to mention his burden for reaching untapped areas like Spain (Romans 15:24,28), it must have been very difficult for Paul to set aside time to write. The importance of writing is rarely obvious to a man of action or to those needing immediate help in their ministries. But God knows well how the written word can be used, and of course, this was no ordinary written material.

The young churches in the first century probably had no way of knowing that their sacrifice in losing access to Paul's gifted genius would result in the production of four marvelous epistles that have ministered to uncounted millions through twenty centuries. The book of Philippians probably would not exist if God had not allowed Paul to be imprisoned at the height of his career.

But this isn't all. He went on to say, "Most of the brethren, trusting in the Lord because of my imprisonment, have far more courage to speak the word of God without fear" (Philippians 1:14). Paul's example was also galvanizing action in the Christian community in Rome.

None of these positive outcomes would have occurred if Paul had adopted an attitude that led him to sit and feel sorry for himself or that viewed the entire episode on a horizontal axis. Those who look at life only on the horizontal axis see other people and events in control and

> *Those who look at life only on the horizontal axis see other people and events in control and cannot see the hand of God at work.*

cannot see the hand of God at work. The horizontal viewpoint is our natural outlook without Christ. Even after conversion, most of us spend far too much of our time looking at the world from a horizontal perspective.

If Paul had viewed his imprisonment on the horizontal level, he would have seen it as the handiwork of anti-Christian Jews and a corrupt and repressive Roman government. Instead of keen eyes for spiritual opportunity, he would have had eyes filled with resentment, bitterness, and mourning for his own misfortune.

We see the vertical perspective at work in the areas of character, teaching, and dialogue in the book of Philippians.

PAUL BEFORE AND AFTER CHRIST

In the book of Acts we get a glimpse of Paul before he knew Christ, and this becomes important for the sake of comparison. Paul first appears when Stephen confounded the men from the "Synagogue of the Freedmen." This was probably Paul's home synagogue. When the council dragged Stephen out to be stoned, they laid their garments at the feet of a man named Saul, who later changed his name to Paul (Acts 7). Then, after Stephen's death, Luke recorded that Paul launched a ferocious persecution of Christians (Acts 8). Paul later admitted that this persecution included not only arresting Christians, but also killing them (Acts 22:4).

What kind of man commits such atrocities? Clearly, Paul was a zealot, but not a reclusive or inward one. He was a crusading driver, a man of exceptional strength. He had described himself in Galatians 1:14 as exceeding his contemporaries in Judaism. In Philippians he went even further, saying,

If anyone else has a mind to put confidence in the flesh, I far more: circumcised the eighth day, of the nation of Israel, of the tribe of Benjamin, a Hebrew of Hebrews; as to the Law, a Pharisee; as to zeal, a persecutor of the church; as to the righteousness which is in the Law, found blameless. (Philippians 3:4-6)

214 ◆ *Grace in Action*

Here was a strong, rigorous man—trained, disciplined, and fierce.

After growing under the hand of God, we see new features in his character. How positive, encouraging, and nurturing he is in the pages of Philippians! His concern for the feelings of Epaphroditus and of the Philippians is wonderfully clear in 2:25-30. His greeting to the Philippians is positive and warm in tone: "For God is my witness, how I long for you all with the affection of Christ Jesus" (1:8). He called them "my dear friends" (2:12, NIV), along with other endearments. Paul was now capable of real compassion and caring love.

THE EXPECTED AND THE UNEXPECTED

This part is the expected. Having lived as a Christian for nearly thirty years, Paul had become a nice person. He was caring and able to nurture. This part of mature Christian character is universally recognized and understood. Any look at a picture of Jesus carrying a lamb suggests the gentle and caring aspect of Christlike character. The One who taught turning the other cheek, and who cared for children, must lead His followers into a life of deep caring.

But there is also the unexpected in Paul's character, even at this late date. Look at the language in 3:2—"Beware of the dogs, beware of the evil workers, beware of the false circumcision." Is it possible that the apostle is calling fellow human beings "dogs"? Are we mistaken in the impression that he is labeling people as "evil workers"?

How could anyone, especially a Christian apostle, justify calling people such names? This seems more like the Paul who killed others before he knew Christ. Yet those of us who believe Scripture is divinely inspired can hardly question whether it was ethical for Paul to speak this way. The fact is, God didn't remove Paul's toughness during the process of spiritual growth. Paul was still aggressive and tough when he needed to be, even after decades in the faith.

There is a lesson here for us. When God transforms the lives of believers, He will not take away basic personality features.

Instead, He will sanctify those features, giving us control over our questionable personality traits while supplying new, complementary traits. Not all Christians will become as aggressive as Paul. This man was so tough he could endure a list of persecutions that seems like a fanciful nightmare, according to 2 Corinthians 11. The Philippians themselves had witnessed him being publicly beaten in their own city square, only to find him singing hymns and praising God later that evening in a dungeon (Acts 16)! This was no ordinary man.

Paul's outrage here, directed toward those who were trying to impose the law on Christian believers (the so-called Judaizers), is phenomenal. Earlier he even suggested that, as long as they had their knives out and sharpened, they ought to carry their zeal for circumcision to the logical conclusion and dismember themselves (Galatians 5:12)! There is a clear note of ribald humor here as well as outrage. Again in this passage in Philippians, he called his enemies the "false circumcision" (*katatome*) but called himself and the other orthodox believers the "true circumcision" (*peritome*). Here the *New American Standard Bible* translators (unlike the *New Interational Version* translators) suddenly become too squeamish to translate frankly a rather profane and humorous comment. Paul made a word play on the word for circumcision (*peri*, to cut around), calling his opponents those who cut—*kata*—off, or in pieces! This is a passionate, and actually rather funny, comment, which might earn him a visit to the board of elders in some of our churches today.

Anyone who menaced the well-being of people in Paul's ministry was in for a fight. Here was someone who wasn't afraid to tell it like it is. Even the Christians in Rome who were preaching for the wrong reasons were candidly denounced in chapter 1 verse 15 and 17: "Some, to be sure, are preaching Christ even from envy and strife . . . out of selfish ambition, rather than from pure motives, thinking to cause me distress in my imprisonment." I think it would have been refreshing to relate to one like Paul, who was forthright, honest, and frank in his opinions, even though this is not what we expect of our Christian leaders today.

In a word, though Paul was a caring person, he was not a sissy. What we see in the character transformation of Paul is that God kept the fiber and strength that had characterized Paul as a nonChristian and added compassion and the ability to care. Paul was still tough, even though he knew how to bear with the weak. Today, this sort of fusion is not always understood. The man or woman of God today is expected to be a hail-fellow-well-met.

> *What we see in the character transformation of Paul is that God kept the fiber and strength that had characterized Paul as a nonChristian and added compassion and the ability to care.*

Ray Stedman once told his nonChristian neighbor that he was going to a pastors' conference. The neighbor cracked a grin and commented that, in his view, attending a pastors' conference would be like sitting in a circle of eunuchs—"You get the feeling something's missing."

Stedman didn't think the joke was funny, but I did. Unfortunately, the image of a Christian leader in our society has become that of a sissy who may not have been able to make it in other lines of work. Some of us have moved far afield in our conceptions of what spiritual maturity looks like.

A MATURE CHRISTIAN WHO WAS FUNNY?

I am so happy that the Paul of these later years had not lost his sense of humor. In Titus, a book written even later in his life, he again lashed out at false teachers, saying, "There are many rebellious men, empty talkers and deceivers, especially those of the circumcision, who must be silenced because they are upsetting whole families, teaching things they should not teach, for the sake of sordid gain" (Titus 1:10-11). This is not exactly a gentle analysis! This could even be considered negative labeling! Today, we would send Paul to a course in political correctness. Apparently, Paul felt that those who were capable of destroying the spiritual health of young Christians didn't deserve gentle treatment.

But he's not done. In verse 12 he cited a Cretan playwright. "One of themselves, a prophet of their own, said, 'Cretans are always liars, evil beasts, lazy gluttons.'" This citation is surprising, but then he said something even more surprising: "This testimony is true. For this cause reprove them severely that they may be sound in the faith" (verse 13).

How could Paul say this harsh testimony about Cretans (that they are always liars, evil beasts, lazy gluttons) was true? It is clearly an overgeneralization, and rather profane. The answer is that Paul had a sense of humor. (I wonder whether he had premeditated the contradiction in saying that a Cretan [the playwright] was telling the truth when he said that Cretans are always liars?) If a smile doesn't come to our face as we read this passage, perhaps we should loosen up a bit.

> *Perhaps God would have some of us change our concept of what He wants us to become. His ideal for our lives might be far less dour and otherworldly than we think.*

Paul must have been a colorful personality. And, if colorful, no doubt his personality was also winsome to the nonChristian. A person who is strong, unafraid, and decisive, yet friendly and funny, would be ideal for reaching lost people with the love of Christ.

VERTICAL PERSPECTIVE: PRAYER DEPENDENCE

Paul shows an exceptional dependence on prayer in his later life. In Philippians 1:3-4 he said, "I thank my God in all my remembrance of you, always offering prayer with joy in my every prayer for you all." He also offered intercessory prayer according to verse 9 and following. But it is interesting that even as he ministered to the Philippians' shortcomings through intercessory prayer, the thanksgiving and joy were always present.

We noted earlier when we studied prayer that the hallmark of prayer offered under the grace paradigm (or the vertical perspective) is thanksgiving. Paul exemplifies the person who prays about the problems of others with the power of God in view. There is ample evidence of conflict and disunity in Philippi, but Paul is not defeated by this knowledge. One like Paul could grapple realistically with problems while remaining aware of God's powerful hand. The result is thanksgiving.

Of course, he prescribed this outlook for the Philippians as well in the well-known passage we already studied in chapter 4, verses 7-8. Philippians has been called the "epistle of joy" because Paul referred to joy and rejoicing so often in spite of his own dire situation and the problems in Philippi.

VERTICAL PERSPECTIVE: CONTENTMENT

Another manifestation of Paul's vertical perspective and the influence it had on his life is his marvelous attitude of content-ment. In what I consider one of the most important passages in the book, he said,

> I have learned to be content in whatever circumstances I am. I know how to get along with humble means, and I also know how to live in prosperity; in any and every circumstance I have learned the secret of being filled and going hungry, both of having abundance and suffer-ing need. I can do all things through Him who strength-ens me. (4:11-13)

Wouldn't this be something! Imagine having the ability to be content in any and every circumstance! This is nothing less than complete victory over our circumstances. Pretending to be content would not bring on this blessed state. Only a deep-seated confidence in God based on years of dealing with Him on the deepest level would ever lead to a perspective that was more or less always content.

The contentment Paul described is not like the passivity of Eastern mysticism, which seeks to end all strife against sup-posed evil or pain. On the contrary, Paul has already said that he presses "on toward the goal for the prize of the upward call of

God in Christ Jesus" (3:14). The contentment Paul felt was not complacency. It was not a feeling that there is nothing more to strive for. It was the sort of contentment that comes from a settled confidence in God's love and power. It was the certain understanding that *all* phases of life are a part of His training of our character. This is the outlook we discussed during our study of the discipline of the Holy Spirit.

VERTICAL PERSPECTIVE: VALUES SYSTEM

According to Paul's discussion of his own life and perspective, his values system had been completely overhauled. Paul had been a Pharisee, and he was trained in Jerusalem by Gamaliel, the leading rabbi of his day. This, in spite of the fact that he was from Tarsus, well outside the boundaries of Palestine, shows that his family had influence. He was also born a Roman citizen. All these facts suggest that Paul was from a wealthy family.

He apparently was either a member or a trainee in the Sanhedrin, which was the highest political office available to Jews at that time. His education was the very best available in the culture of his day. As a rabbi-Pharisee from Jerusalem, with money and political power, and a Roman citizen to boot, Paul stood at the top of the social order. He had it all.

After describing many of these benefits in his former life, he said in 3:7-8,

> But whatever things were gain to me, those things I have counted as loss for the sake of Christ. More than that, I count all things to be loss in view of the surpassing value of knowing Christ Jesus my Lord, for whom I have suffered the loss of all things, and count them but rubbish in order that I may gain Christ.

Like the person who has seen through his obsession with collecting forks, Paul simply could not attach importance to the prestige values of his day. He had been mentally transformed by the renewing of his mind, not conformed to the world system.

A person with a vertical perspective like Paul's cannot continue to hold to a horizontal value system.

In what is likely the last letter Paul wrote, he admitted to his intimate friend, Timothy, "I am already being poured out as a drink offering, and the time of my departure has come" (2 Timothy 4:6). This time, unlike when he wrote Philippians, Paul knew for sure he had reached the end of his earthly life. Looking back, he was able to reveal how his values system worked: "I have fought the good fight, I have finished the course, I have kept the faith; in the future there is laid up for me the crown of righteousness, which the Lord, the righteous Judge, will award to me on that day; and not only to me, but also to all who have loved His appearing" (2 Timothy 4:7-8). To anyone who truly believes in the afterlife, a values system based on the temporal is sheer nonsense.

> *A person with a vertical perspective like Paul's cannot continue to hold to a horizontal value system.*

VERTICAL PERSPECTIVE: WILLINGNESS TO SUFFER

In place of his former quest for prestige, Paul now felt a willingness to suffer for the sake of spiritual transformation. He expressed this when he shared his desire "that I may know Him, and the power of His resurrection and the fellowship of His sufferings, being conformed to His death; in order that I may attain to the resurrection from the dead" (Philippians 3:10-11). Paul was not worried about failing to make it to Heaven unless he suffered enough. When he talked about "conform[ity] to His death" and "attain[ing] to the resurrection," he was referring to his desire to see his *condition* reflect his *position*. Just as we saw earlier, there is both a building-up and a tearing-down action needed in the lives of Christians. When Paul said he wanted to "attain to the resurrection from the dead," he meant *in this life*, not in the next.

This should be obvious from verse 12: "Not that I have already obtained it." If resurrection from the dead referred to going to Heaven, this statement would be ridiculous. He obviously couldn't have obtained Heaven because he was still alive! No, this is referring to the same transformation referred to in passages like 2 Corinthians 4:11, where Paul described himself as "constantly being delivered over to death for Jesus' sake, that the life of Jesus also may be manifested in our mortal flesh."

Paul again demonstrated in the book of Philippians his readiness to undergo suffering if it meant he could manifest more truly the life of Jesus to others.

VERTICAL PERSPECTIVE: EVANGELISTIC ZEAL

Paul never lost his evangelistic zeal, like so many older Christians do. We have already seen in Philippians 1 that he was constantly witnessing to soldiers who guarded him. Of course, Paul was a gifted evangelist. But his concern for evangelism did not grow out of his gifting. It grew directly out of his vertical perspective and his eternity-oriented values system. Because his relationship with God had become so real to him, his certainty about the afterlife was unshakable. This led unavoidably to a deep-seated burden for the lost.

In another letter written at the same time, Paul exhorted the Colossians to devote themselves to prayer,

> Praying at the same time for us as well, that God may open up to us a door for the word, so that we may speak forth the mystery of Christ, for which I have also been imprisoned; in order that I may make it clear in the way I ought to speak. Conduct yourselves with wisdom toward outsiders, making the most of the opportunity. Let your speech always be with grace, seasoned, as it were, with salt, so that you may know how you should respond to each person. (Colossians 4:3-6)

Remember, this statement was made while the apostle was in prison. It seems that Paul could never stop thinking about the lost. Whether it was because of his new spiritually bestowed ability to care for others or his value system based on the eternal perspective, it all added up to the same thing to Paul. His life and the lives of other Christians ought to be expended on the task of evangelism.

Reformed theologians believe Paul held to unconditional election. But even the strongest Calvinist knows that if God has ordained the ends, He has also ordained the means to those ends. One thing is clear: Nothing in Paul's theology allowed him to become complacent about the ocean of lost people around him. If we are to imitate Paul, our lives should also reflect this unceasing burden for the lost. This friend of God was also the friend of the lost.

ONE OTHER FEATURE
The description of Paul's person and character as seen in Philippians and other books written near the end of his life is challenging and attractive. All Christians who thirst to be close to God must look at Paul's life with envy and perhaps despair. But it would be a big mistake to miss one of the most important autobiographical notes in this book.

In chapter 3 verses 12 through 14 he said,

> Not that I have already obtained [conformity to Christ's
> death and resurrection], or have already become perfect,
> but I press on in order that I may lay hold of that for
> which also I was laid hold of by Christ Jesus. Brethren, I
> do not regard myself as having laid hold of it yet; but
> one thing I do: forgetting what lies behind and reaching
> forward to what lies ahead, I press on toward the goal
> for the prize of the upward call of God in Christ Jesus.

This is more like it. After nearly three decades of the most intensive spiritual growth and training, including personal bodily visits from Christ and at least one tour of Heaven (2 Corinthians 12:3-4), Paul still was not able to say he had it all together. His progress was impressive, but he was still acutely aware of his own weaknesses. It is a sign of growth in grace when we become increasingly aware of our unworthiness, sin, and failure, while at the same time also learning to trust God more fully. Clearly, it is possible to be aware of, but not focused on, our sin and failures.

WHAT IS LEFT FOR US?

Why not do as Paul did? First, he says he forgets what lies behind. This means, in both the positive and the negative sense, the past can hold us down because we base our identity on it. Many Christians are plagued by defeat because they are constantly comparing their current experience to some golden period in the past when it seemed like they were close to God. Compared to that time, everything else is pale by contrast. But Paul says he forgets what lies behind. The joys and victories we once experienced were for that time only. They are not for today. Now, God has a different path for us, and we should apply ourselves to finding and walking that path, not trying to relive something that is now over.

So, too, with negative experiences. Some Christians can't break free from sins they have committed in the past. I have counseled women who cannot look away from the time they had an abortion. Some men cannot forgive themselves for committing adultery. By accusing them, the Evil One is able to keep them in defeat for years because of this sin. Still others cannot stop focusing on how they have been victimized by others. Past betrayals and evils can keep us from what God wants us to experience if we cannot "forget what lies behind."

If Paul wrote that statement today, he would probably be charged with advocating denial. But this is not denial. Paul knew what he had done. He knew he had murdered Christians. He knew he had been a powerful, wealthy man. He simply chose to relegate these things to where they belonged: the past. They could not help him or hinder him now that he was a new creature in Christ.

Instead of focusing on the past, he says he "reaches forward to what lies ahead." What is this? This is the vertical perspective! It is to his identity in Christ, and to Christ Himself, that Paul looks.

Paul calls on us directly to follow the same path he did. In Philippians 3:15-16 he says, "Let us therefore, as many as are perfect [mature], have this attitude; and if in anything you have a different attitude, God will reveal that also to you; however, let us keep living by that same standard to which we have attained." What beautiful security and grace there is in this imperative. Paul calls us to adopt an attitude relative to the level we have attained so far. God is not going to ask us to do something we are not able to do.

On the other hand, if we are stubbornly refusing to follow God by continuing to entertain negative attitudes, we have one of the most precious promises in the New Testament here: "God will reveal that also to you." Even people like me, who are sometimes disobedient, have the assurance here that God is not going to forsake us. He will reveal our problematic attitude to us. Then we will have the opportunity to repent from our hearts and follow Him again.

It is to us today that Paul calls:

Brethren, join in following my example, and . . . walk according to the pattern you have in us. (Philippians 3:17)

THE INDICATIVE AND IMPERATIVE MOODS

The terms *indicative* and *imperative* refer to two different verb moods commonly used by the New Testament authors in their teaching on sanctification.[1]

WHAT IS A VERB MOOD?

The mood of a verb designates the relationship of the verb's action to reality. The following is a simple list of verb moods in the New Testament and what they generally signify:

- Indicative—mood of certainty, actuality
- Subjunctive—mood of probability
- Optative—mood of possibility
- Imperative—mood of command

The New Testament uses indicative statements when discussing what God has done, is doing, or will do. Imperative statements are used when saying what we should do. It is important to realize that not only are both moods present in the Bible, but that there is a specific relationship between them in the area of sanctification. Namely, what God commands us to do (the imperative) is based upon what He has done, is doing, or will do (the indicatives). God is signifying by this consistent pattern that sanctification depends on Him but involves human volition and cooperation.

EXAMPLES
Romans 6:1-19 and 8:1-13 are two of the best examples of this relationship, but we have already covered them. Here are some others. In these passages, the imperative statements are in bold type, while the indicative statements are in italics.

Philippians 2:12-13

Work out your salvation with fear and trembling; *for it is God who works in you to will and to act according to his good purpose.* (NIV)

In this example, we see that the imperative command to work out our salvation is based on the fact that God is at work in us. The use of the word *for* indicates dependence or causality.

Colossians 3:1-17

Since, then, you have been raised with Christ, **set your hearts on things above, where Christ is seated at the right hand of God. Set your minds on things above, not on earthly things.** *For you died, and your life is now hidden with Christ in God. When Christ, who is your life, appears, then you also will appear with him in glory.*
    Put to death, therefore, whatever belongs to your earthly nature: sexual immorality, impurity, lust, evil desires and greed, which is idolatry. *Because of these, the wrath of God is coming.* You used to walk in these ways, in the life you once lived. **But now you must rid yourselves of all such things as these: anger, rage, malice, slander, and filthy language from your lips.**

Do not lie to each other, *since you have taken off your old self with its practices and have put on the new self, which is being renewed in knowledge in the image of its Creator. Here there is no Greek or Jew, circumcised or uncircumcised, barbarian, Scythian, slave or free, but Christ is all, and is in all.*

Therefore, as God's chosen people, holy and dearly loved, clothe yourselves with compassion, kindness, humility, gentleness and patience. Bear with each other and forgive whatever grievances you may have against one another. Forgive *as the Lord forgave you.* **And over all these virtues put on love, which binds them all together in perfect unity.**

Let the peace of Christ rule in your hearts, *since as members of one body you were called to peace.* **And be thankful. Let the word of Christ dwell in you richly as you teach and admonish one another with all wisdom, and as you sing psalms, hymns and spiritual songs with gratitude in your hearts to God. And whatever you do, whether in word or deed, do it all in the name of the Lord Jesus, giving thanks to God the Father through him.** (NIV)

Again, by looking at the linkage between the statements (for example, words like *since, for, as,* and *because*), you will notice that the imperatives are dependent on indicative statements. When we consider the thought development in this passage, we realize Paul is at pains to regularly remind his readers of the basis for each ethical instruction.

Hebrews 10:19-25

Therefore, brothers, *since we have confidence to enter the Most Holy Place by the blood of Jesus, by a new and living way opened for us through the curtain, that is, his body,* and *since we have a great priest over the house of*

God, **let us draw near to God with a sincere heart in full assurance of faith, having our hearts sprinkled to cleanse us from a guilty conscience and having our bodies washed with pure water. Let us hold unswervingly to the hope we profess, for he who promised is faithful. And let us consider how we may spur one another on toward love and good deeds. Let us not give up meeting together, as some are in the habit of doing, but let us encourage one another—and all the more as you see the Day approaching.** (NIV)

In this passage, no fewer than five separate imperatives are tied to two wonderful indicatives: our confidence to enter the Holy Place by the new way, and our great High Priest. Notice the word *since* before both indicative statements, indicating that they provide the basis for the imperatives to follow.

Ephesians 4:32

Be kind and compassionate to one another, forgiving each other, *just as in Christ God forgave you.* (NIV)

It is because God has forgiven us that we should forgive others. Compare this to Matthew 6:14-15, where God's forgiveness is conditional on our forgiving others. The formulation in Matthew is typical of the Sermon on the Mount, which teaches the true nature of the law. There, the imperative is the *condition* for God's forgiveness, not a response to it.

DYNAMIC RELATIONSHIP
The New Testament also teaches that, although the imperatives are based upon the indicatives, in many cases the *experience* of the indicatives is dependent upon our willingness to respond to the imperatives by faith. In other words, if I fail to act in faith based on what God has commanded, I may not experience the reality of my position in Christ. Of course, my

position is no less real, but I may not experience it in the way God wants me to.

This corrects a common misconception among Christians: that even after we have understood God's promises, we should wait until we experience God's power, forgiveness, etc., before we act on what He says to do. On the contrary, we must act in the knowledge of the indicatives before we actually sense or experience the truth. Thus, the biblical order is not LEARN-EXPERIENCE-ACT, but rather LEARN-ACT-EXPERIENCE. This also corrects the erroneous position that man's response is not important in sanctification. Of course, our experience is also important, especially when it is understood in its proper place.

Examples: You may enjoy examining this relationship in the following passages: John 13:17; Romans 6:15; 8:4-13; 12:1; Galatians 5:16-23; James 1:21-24; 1 Peter 2:2,9-12; 3:7; 2 Peter 1:3-9; 1 John 3:14,18-19; 4:19.

NOTE
1. This appendix is adapted from a paper I coauthored with my colleague, Gary DeLashmutt.